"Guy Finley embodies universal wisdom. With his compassionate heart, Guy teaches practical insights each of us can apply in our daily lives to realize our own divinity."

Philip M. Hellmich, director of peace at the Shift Network and author of *God and Conflict: A Search for Peace in a Time of Crisis*

"Finley gives us some exquisite keys to help us look deeply into who we are in this present moment, what we are truly longing for, and how to live from our best self."

Justine Toms, co-founder and host of New Dimensions Radio and author of *Small Pleasures: Finding Grace in a Chaotic World*

"The deep and meaningful content found in *The Secret of Your Immortal Self* will guide you to shed self-limitation and fear, and awaken you to steadfast clarity, intuition, and wisdom. This is your opportunity for transformation. Let Guy support you with this remarkable book."

Jennifer McLean, creator of Body Dialog Healing and host of "Healing with the Masters"

"Guy Finley's *Secret of Your Immortal Self* helps unlock the doorway to your inner Self. Guy writes in a manner that is both poetic and practical. I highly recommend this book to anyone seeking truth."

Nayaswami Jyotish, spiritual director of Ananda Sangha and author of *How to Meditate*

"Guy Finley offers us a roadmap into the most important journey we can take. In a simple but profoundly eloquent way, Finley helps us see who we really are: a divine being that is boundless and eternal."

Servet Hasan, author of the International Book Awards Winner *Life in Transition: An Intuitive Guide to New Beginnings*

"Filled with ideas worthy of deep contemplation and practices you can use daily, these essays will help turn you in the direction of self-realization—the true goal in life that will bring you to the state of deep inner joy you are seeking."

Krysta Gibson, publisher, *New Spirit Journal*

THE
Secret
OF YOUR
Immortal
Self

THE
Secret
OF YOUR
Immortal
Self

Key Lessons for Realizing
the Divinity Within

GUY FINLEY

Llewellyn Publications
WOODBURY, MINNESOTA

FIRST EDITION
First Printing, 2015

Book design and edit by Rebecca Zins
Cover design by Ellen Lawson
Cover photo by iStockphoto.com/3002495/©fotoVoyager
Interior Rocky Mountain maple tree image © 2004 Dover Publications
(from *Trees & Leaves CD-ROM & Book*)

Llewellyn is a registered trademark of Llewellyn Worldwide Ltd.

Library of Congress Cataloging-in-Publication Data
Finley, Guy, 1949–
  The secret of your immortal self : key lessons for realizing the divinity within /
Guy Finley.—FIRST EDITION.
     pages cm
   ISBN 978-0-7387-4407-0
   1. Spiritual life. I. Title.
   BL624.F51645 2015
   204'.4—dc23

2014032994

Llewellyn Worldwide does not participate in, endorse, or have any authority or responsibility concerning private business transactions between our authors and the public.

  All mail addressed to the author is forwarded, but the publisher cannot, unless specifically instructed by the author, give out an address or phone number.

  Any Internet references contained in this work are current at publication time, but the publisher cannot guarantee that a specific location will continue to be maintained. Please refer to the publisher's website for links to authors' websites and other sources.

Llewellyn Publications
A Division of Llewellyn Worldwide Ltd.
2143 Wooddale Drive
Woodbury, MN 55125-2989

www.llewellyn.com

Printed in the United States of America

Other Books by Guy Finley
The Secret of Letting Go

The Seeker, The Search, The Sacred

The Courage to Be Free

The Essential Laws of Fearless Living

Let Go and Live in the Now

Freedom from the Ties That Bind

Design Your Destiny

*Breaking Dependency: Learning to
Let Go from the Inside Out*

Audio Albums
Seven Steps to Oneness

The Meditative Life

Secrets of Being Unstoppable

Being Fearless and Free

*For the Love of Life: Seeing the Good
When Things Look Bad*

The Meaning of Life

Forever Free

DVD Albums

Life Is Real Only When You Are

Wisdom's Path to the Happiness Within

For a complete list of over 200 inspired works
by Guy Finley, visit www.guyfinley.org,
where you can also sign up to receive
free weekly insights by email.

CONTENTS

A Sneak Peak at What You'll Find in This Book

There is no reward on earth, or even amongst the stars, equal to the realization of the divinity within you. Those who have awakened and attained this pearl of great value understand—with no sense of pride for their knowledge—that the greatest of human beings is nothing compared to the least of those who have realized the immortal Self. In their soul burns a light that will never go out, a strength that no fear can shake, and a wisdom that understands, without taking thought, that all things good come to those for whom the good is all things.

In one sense, the interior journey that leads to the immortal Self is demanding and difficult, even seemingly impossible at times; and yet, as paradoxical as it seems, there is nothing intrinsically hard about rising above ourselves and slipping into the stream of our own celestial possibilities. After all, how hard is it to let go of a favorite pair of shoes that no longer fit or a sweater worn so thin that it no longer stops even the slightest breeze? These things, beloved as they may have been, have *outlived their purpose.*

The realization of the immortal Self is inseparable from seeing that who and what we have been in the past—our flattering self-images, treasured ideas, and most prized opinions—no longer serve us. And how do we know when the time has come to drop the very things that once defined our lives? When we see that holding on to them causes suffering.

Much as a great hot air balloon rises into the open skies the moment its restraining tether is cut, so does the aspirant begin his or her ascent into the everlasting life in much the same way. One action: letting go.

Two results: we leave one world—one level of self—behind us and, in the same moment, rise into a higher order of our own consciousness.

Here, in this book's first key lesson, is a summary of this great spiritual law. It also provides a sneak peak into what you are about to learn.

KEY LESSON

Growing into the worlds above us—realizing the higher realms of consciousness within us—requires that we outgrow the worlds beneath us.

INTRODUCTION

Look Into the Invisible Mirror of the Immortal Self

How I Came to Write This Book

A long time ago, nearly fifty years now, I was walking through an open market in a small upscale beach town. Colorful booths of various sizes were displaying the works of local artisans. The late summer afternoon was warm and beautiful, refreshed by a cooling sea breeze that washed away any gathering heat. I was content just to be there, taking in all the sights and sounds. Besides, nothing is more pleasurable to an inveterate treasure hunter than the hope he might just stumble upon something no one else has seen or wants. And then it happened.

In my mind's eye, I can still see the thirty odd, old, small wooden benches. They were of differing heights and laid out in three parallel lines with space allowed to walk between them. Upon them sat dozens upon dozens of diminutive trees.

I had heard of bonsai trees before but had never actually seen a living specimen. Each tree was a miniature version of a towering pine, elm, or oak. And, stranger still, each little tree was planted in a small, ancient-looking pot that appeared way too shallow to support it, let alone allow the tree to thrive. I was spellbound; the next thing I knew—like a moth to the proverbial flame—I was drawn into the center of their display. And then something even more inexplicable took place.

As I stood over the first bench before me, my eyes became fixed on some kind of pine tree that stood less than twenty inches tall but had the appearance of being over a hundred years old! Its weathered, ancient trunk—turned almost back in upon itself—radiated a silent story; it told of a solitary life alone upon some steep sea cliff where, buffeted by unrelenting winds, its character had been shaped by the hardships it was given to bear. And with this one impression, an overwhelming emotion came rolling over me like a wave from some unknown sea within my heart, and I started to cry.

I knew full well that I was in a public place, yet I was powerless to contain my feelings, so powerful was the impression received from this one tree—not to mention the feeling of being surrounded by a miniature forest of other perfect specimens. The beauty of it all outweighed any concern of being seen as a fool or a madman.

The rest of that afternoon was spent in a private audience before each of these ancient trees. I was eager to hear their individual stories. There was no way to explain it back then, but now I understand at least some of the real reasons behind this uncanny attraction, including the strong emotional reaction that came on its heels.

As the following explanation reveals, everything points to the existence of a timeless interior Presence that doesn't just precede the relationships we are drawn to in our lives but actually serves to arrange them, including whatever life lessons we take from these encounters. Calling on our own past experience will help validate the truth of this last idea, as well as reveal some of the possibilities it holds for those willing to explore its extraordinary implications.

Within each of us lives a tireless, latent longing to touch—and be touched by—life's invisible celestial forces. For instance, whenever we stand as a silent witness to the endless expanse of a dark night sky, we are inwardly moved by this outer display of timelessness spread out above us.

We can't help being drawn to look at a newborn child because the innocence we see within those eyes stirs the depths of our own heart, reminding us of a vital but now largely forgotten virtue. Again, drinking in these exterior impressions awakens, moves, and reminds us of something still latent within us.

Which brings us to this very important point: each and every one of these precious impressions—taken in from around us, regardless of its nature—does more than just touch us: *it reveals us to ourselves; it actually serves to tell us something about our innermost self that can't be heard or felt in any other way.*

In other words, anything that is reflected upon the mirror of one's soul—be it a majestic mountain, a single red rose, or a smile on the face of someone we love—creates a kind of instant and corresponding recognition within us. And through this higher self-awareness, our new eyes see the truth that sets us free: the supposed "other" person, that stirring moment, or whatever experiences we are drawn to reflect within us—none of these are really "other" at all. Everything we can realize in this life or in any kingdom come is already an indwelling part of our consciousness—and always has been!

The unshakable self-knowledge this understanding provides is the secret wellspring of all spiritual mystics, saints, and sages; it is their undying source of wisdom, compassion, and strength, regardless of whatever religious tradition they may have come to represent in passing time.

My one wish—held since before the age of twelve and, beyond any doubt, the seed of all my experiences leading up to writing this book—is that the day comes when all of us drink from these living waters and then follow them all the way back home to their immortal source within us. What I have written here—the knowledge that I share with you—*is always just the beginning*; it is as new as we are willing to let it act upon us. In this way, each awakening is the first step in the greatest journey that any of us will ever undertake.

The Gifts This Book Will Give to You

For those who seek a deeper, more meaningful relationship with the Divine or who want to let go of the misery of useless suffering, *The Secret of Your Immortal Self* opens the doors to a new level of understanding that makes both wishes come true *at the same time*. This book provides powerful insights and practical steps on how to find a guiding light in the middle of any dark moment—a light that both reveals the illusion of imagined self-limitation and instantly releases you from the fear of it.

Each of these unique essays helps the reader remember a long-forgotten part of their true, timeless nature. Piece by piece, this recollection stirs the sleeping soul that, once awakened, guides the individual to the crowning moment of life: contact with the immortal Self.

The gifts of this celestial union and the new order of self conceived through it provide more than can ever be imagined. This authentic "second birth" releases the aspirant from all forms of regret, endows him or her with a patience and compassion that no enemy can provoke, and, perhaps most important of all, grants the realization that—despite all appearances to the contrary—*death is not the end of life.*

In your hands is much more than just a collection of writings; the insights revealed on each and every page come to you from another world that already dwells within you.

Each essay illuminates a separate facet of the immortal Self. Some reveal and deal with unseen dark parts of our nature dedicated to keeping us spiritually asleep, while still others offer insights, encouragements, and signposts along the way, all designed to help speed our journey of spiritual awakening.

The short stories you'll find interspersed between these essays are written as spiritual parables; they're meant to touch mind and heart at the same time. To receive the greatest benefit from their special lessons, read each story with the understanding that *all their unique characters live within you;* their circumstances, words, and actions all represent some level of self, some quality or character whose nature we must witness within us before we can realize the immortal Self. Use these stories like mirrors; reflect upon them by being willing to see yourself in them.

As you'll see, some essays and stories will be more attractive to you than others. Remember, their intended purpose is to stir within you what cannot be touched by anything else. This feeling of attraction is actually an invitation; it comes to you from higher possibilities still latent within you. Think of how naturally you give your complete attention to something beautiful in nature—of how it calls out to you to share in its life and how you can't wait to lend yourself to that end—and then realize this exact same principle holds true when it comes to seeing and experiencing something eternal within you when it is first stirred in your consciousness.

Take your time with each of these writings. You would never rush through a field of wildflowers because you know everywhere, anywhere you look, there awaits something for you to see that is more breathtaking than the moment before. So, whether you read this book page by page, as you would a novel, or open it randomly, looking for a needed answer or insight to a question in mind, allow each essay and story to share its secret with you. Listen to the subsequent stirrings of your heart as you would a close friend who you know wants to tell you something about yourself that you don't just need to hear but that you *want* to hear because of the positive impact you know it will make in your life.

One last thought: your willingness to quietly contemplate whatever calls to you from within these pages will lead you to the source of that higher consciousness that initiated the call. Let yourself be drawn inward, and then dare to act on the truths that you're being given to see.

Accordingly, and to help you start incorporating this new knowledge you're about to receive, I've written a special key lesson at the end of each writing. Use these condensed lessons as your point of focus; meditate on their insights, and watch how your eyes will be opened to realize more deeply the core elements of the message that they're designed help summarize. Give yourself freely to what you are given to see, and you cannot fail to reach and realize the innermost source of yourself.

Let Go and Awaken to a Whole New You

By the fact that everything about her existence is perfectly ordered, Mother Nature is choiceless. What does being without choice mean in this context? All creatures, from the smallest to the largest—from gnat to gorilla and all the way to the humpback whale—must serve nature as she demands. Their individual lives exist to serve and sustain a living planetary matrix greater than themselves.

One of the gifts of being human is that our individual potential far exceeds the boundaries of our (animal) body, which, like all natural creations, must serve the general laws it's been created to obey. We have the possibility of consciously knowing the existence of another order of body that is in, but not of our physical form. For example, consider the oak tree; it is in the acorn, yet its body is timeless relative to the seed from which it emerges.

To see the truth of this principle in the life of a simple seed and tree as an earthly, or lower, expression of higher laws is more than just promising; it is spiritually empowering. *This exact same law holds true when it comes to the nature of our own consciousness.* Within our present level of being—think of it as a seed relative to the tree that will rise out of it—dwells a timeless level of ourselves that isn't subject to the laws of the natural world. This higher level of self, much like the life of a tree as compared to its seed, is relatively immortal—and, as such, *it is created to serve another order of existence.*

This extraordinary possibility of being "born again"—of achieving Nirvana or Moksha—is seeded into us from the beginning, yet no seed is the flowering it promises unless it's cultivated and nourished. And this is precisely where the inner work of the willing aspirant must be brought into play. Spiritual rebirth is not evolutionary, even though the cosmos moves and perfects itself to assist as a midwife. The second birth is realized through an act of free will; *it is voluntary, not mandatory.*

In order to nurture our own awakening, we must first see the need to let go of those parts of us that we sense no longer serve us. This new kind of self-awareness is the interior "seed state" needed to outgrow and transcend our former level of self. But these seeds of higher self-knowledge must, in turn, become new actions if they are to awaken us to our immortal Self.

Consider the following four separate instructions that follow as a single seed and the course of action needed for the flowering of a whole new you. Let them guide you to an incorruptible consciousness that is as timeless as the greater good from which it comes.

> *Remember yourself:* Be as present as possible within yourself—to the whole of yourself— at all times.
>
> *Receive and accept whatever is revealed as the gift that it is:* There is no such thing

as a bad fact for those who seek spiritual freedom.

Release yourself: Refuse to judge, justify, blame, or console yourself.

Endure yourself: Never forget the following: There are two kinds of suffering. One is born of not wanting to see or be what life reveals about your present nature. This is useless, unconscious suffering; it serves only to reincarnate a level of self that always rejects unwanted revelations about itself. *The other kind of suffering is the conscious sacrifice of this nature.* It is our agreement to let go of who and what we have been in order to make way for the birth of a new and timeless order of being.

*Spiritually speaking, all relationships serve
one purpose: self-knowledge. Self-knowledge
serves one purpose: awakening to the truth of
oneself. Awakening to the truth of oneself serves
one purpose: dying to oneself. Dying to oneself
serves one purpose: rebirth. And rebirth is the
purpose and fulfillment of all relationships.*

Realize the Crowning Moment of Life

The crowning moment of any species, the culmination of its possibilities, *can't* be just its ability to adapt and survive. Natural history demonstrates that entire populations peak and are then terminated whenever Mother Nature so decides. The great book of life simply closes out one chapter of creation after another once it no longer serves the need for which it was created. Nothing can resist these decisions, which are reached in a higher order of reality than the one they act upon.

To the casual eye, the extinction of a species, for whatever reason, seems like it takes a very long time.

But a closer look at this process tells another story. Our scale of time is skewed by the short span of life we are each allotted on this earth. In truth, compared to the lifespan of our planet, an entire species—let alone an individual within it—can vanish virtually overnight.

When we view life through this kind of sweeping perspective, it may be hard to see how such a grand scale of life has anything to do with our individual lives. So let's examine these ideas and make them very personal and specific to your life and mine.

For instance, of what use is our endless struggle to adapt and even achieve some of the more common culturally valued prizes knowing—as we all do—that nothing we can ever possess has the power to stave off our inevitable passing?

The following quotation from Vernon Howard, a great twentieth-century mystic, not only helps put this stark idea into proper perspective for us but, as we will see, also hints at a far more appealing possibility as well:

> *"It is wise to seek immortality, for time defeats all other ambitions."*

True spiritual gems such as this are scattered throughout time, found mostly in the forgotten treasure troves of authentic sacred writings. In the beautiful light they reflect is hidden a promise that is as welcome and timeless as our need to be reminded of it:

Within each of us already lives a higher order of being, an immortal spirit that neither time nor circumstance can cause to end.

Seated at the center of each of us lies buried a kind of celestial seed, buried there since the beginning of time. But this divine gift must be awakened—in this lifetime—before its fruit can be realized, for it alone contains life's greatest prize: *victory over death*—a conscious connection to a vine everlasting that never dies. The expression of this fruition is inseparable from our freedom from the fear of death, even as our freedom from death is the same as finally fulfilling our highest individual possibilities.

The true purpose for the incarnation of Christ or any other authentic avatar, saint, prophet, or sage—regardless of his or her place and time of birth—is a single purpose expressed through two phases. First, to remind us of our lost heritage: we are children of a Celestial Being and within us dwells the seed of an immortal Self. And second, upon awakening to this forgotten heritage, to accept the responsibility that comes with it: to use our lives to help manifest the will of heaven on earth so that these two planes of existence, and their beings, may be reconciled and perfected accordingly.

The higher order of unconditional love and compassion, as evidenced by the selfless lives of saints and sages—acting as heralds of a heaven to come—proves the existence of a higher order of being awakened in them but still asleep within us. As such, the knowledge they disseminate is designed to help us awaken this celestial consciousness within us, much as sunlight acts upon a dormant seed, stirring it to open. All true spiritual masters are in concert when it comes to this last vital revelation; it is perhaps the greatest spiritual "secret" on this earth.

For any "flower" to live, the seed of its origin must die. It is a law: the latter must pass before the former can prosper and reveal its latent potential. Virtually all scripture, East and West, affirms this sacred teaching as expressed here by Christ:

"Verily, verily, I say unto you, Except a corn of wheat fall into the ground and die, it abideth alone: but if it die, it bringeth forth much fruit."

The hidden meaning of this oft-quoted, little-understood phrase is as follows: the "corn of wheat" in this passage represents the spiritually asleep, unawakened human. The seed, in both instances, is just the first stage of its being; it is a herald of possibilities yet to be realized. As such, as is true with any seed, physical or spiritual, if it doesn't succeed with its ordained task or somehow rejects its natural role, the very reason for its existence is rendered null and void.

We hold within us a sublime seed richly impregnated with divine possibilities; it is our greatest gift. Within it lives the promise of an immortal Self, a celestial citizenship in a world outside the prison and pain of passing time. But again—as is true of all seeds, regardless of their nature—each must find the right conditions and nourishment needed for it to flourish. Once accomplished, almost nothing can stop this seed from breaking free and stepping out of its confining husk. In that instant it is reborn into a new form; it enters into the next level of its being, and the journey begins anew.

KEY LESSON

The rose that opens in the summer sun
glorifies its creator; in its crowning moment
it does not care about those who walk
by, failing to notice its beauty, nor does
it blush for any praise it receives.

Find the Secret Entrance
Into the Life Immortal

There is no "right" road to follow that leads to the realization of one's immortal Self.

If we wish to be one with a celestial consciousness, capable of responding with effortless wisdom to any demand—regardless of its nature, high or low—then all images of such a being must be thrown away. St. Paul provides us with the reason why we must agree to die to those parts of us that hope for a higher life to come:

> "But hope that is seen is no hope at all. Who hopes for what he already has?"

The life divine, in its ceaseless revelation of creation, is inimitable; so we must be, too. To spiritually model oneself after anything or anyone—no matter how sublime—is imitation, and any form such imitation assumes, regardless of how sincere, is by its very nature antithetical to revelation.

The illumined poet T. S. Eliot strengthens this same finding:

> *"I said to my soul, be still, and wait without hope, for hope would be hope for the wrong thing; wait without love, for love would be love of the wrong thing; there is yet faith, but the faith and the love and the hope are all in the waiting. Wait without thought, for you are not ready for thought: So the darkness shall be the light, and the stillness the dancing."*

The realization of one's immortal Self is inseparable from its revelation. What is timeless isn't in a time to come; it is merely hidden within passing time, much as the sky often goes unnoticed because of the clouds that sail through its vast, open spaces. This exact same relationship holds true when it comes to you and what is divine. To ask yourself, "What must I do in order to be all that I am?" amounts to something like the eye asking, "What must I do to be able to see?"

Again, the true spiritual life is incomparable; nothing comes before revelation of the living now, and nothing follows it. Dare to be—to see just what you are in each moment revealed; give yourself to this task wholeheartedly. Your willing entrance into the whole estate of yourself is the same as entering into the unattainable life you seek.

KEY LESSON

At its best, imitation is limitation. At its worst, imitation is the corruption of one's own God-given uniqueness.

The Winds of Faith

When the soul cries out to spirit to carry her to a new world beyond the boundaries of this earthly domain, she is calling for the winds of faith to sweep down, fill her tattered and empty sails, and take her safely away. The wait for these winds is never too long for any soul who is both patient and persistent in purpose.

And when—as it must come to pass upon any such journey home—dark, uncharted waters begin breaking over the sloping bow of her deck and no calm anchorage is anywhere in sight—the soul, now being swept across the deep of unknown seas, must keep in her heart the remembrance of two things: she cannot know her destination, and she must surrender the helm of her vessel and agree to follow the winds that she has invoked to transport her there.

KEY LESSON

The great journey leading to the immortal Self does not begin with fact but in faith untested. It is the journey of faith alone that reveals the fact of the Divine, much as a flower proves the unseen seed from which it springs into the light.

It's Impossible to Hide and
See at the Same Time

Too often the press reports a sad story about some famous person who has taken his or her own life. Any act of self-destruction, whether by drug abuse, alcoholism, or through some shorter route, is always tragic news; it avails no one save for the media that likes to serve this kind of misery to the public in order to feed itself. But for the aspirant who wishes to awaken from the dream of this life, reports such as these can serve a much different and higher purpose. Within them are hidden, important truths about our world, what it values, and how innocent minds are made victims of unseen forces within and around them at all times. As such, we must work to see through the usual "smoke and mirror" explanations of these tragedies and learn to read between the lines. Only in this way can the sadness and waste of human life be transformed into something promising and eventually good for all.

What is the true underlying story when we see a "star" come crashing down to earth and come to such an inglorious end? The answer is right before our eyes. Truth be told, very few of us go through our lives without the thought that the pain of being alive isn't worth the cost. The reason for the visitation of this on-and-off again sense of futility and the despair it breeds is as follows:

> *There is a direct and proportionate relationship between the degree of inconsolable pain that we have and a deep-seated misunderstanding of our real purpose for being alive.*

A moment's examination of the above explanation helps prove its validity. After all, what does one do when, having fulfilled one's imagined purpose—including acquiring everything once hoped for—one still feels empty? Where else does one turn when the known roads to happiness have been exhausted? All of us have known these moments where there seems to be no escape or viable solution to our growing sense of discontent. In the case of celebrities, and in the many other unpublished stories like these, this seemingly unanswerable despair leads to acts of desperation that are ultimately self-destructive.

The shock of such stories, as is almost always the case when we learn of some beloved celebrity taking his or her life, is that we're predisposed—even readily deceived—into believing that a person's manicured appearance is the same as his actual character. How many times have you heard someone say something like, "I can't believe it! He was such a happy-go-lucky person," or something to that effect? This general sense of disbelief has a specific cause common to our present level of consciousness. The real reason that we believe in any public performance—be it that of some well-known star or our own friends and loved ones—is that we are all, to one extent or another, actors on a stage.

It's not too far from the mark to say that many of us have come to believe that being a good performer in life is somehow the same as fulfilling the purpose of life. Here's the strange logic behind the self-created misery that follows it:

For each successful "performance" we pull off around others or within ourselves, it feels as if we've won, for the moment, what we've imagined will make us whole and happy—but the drawback here should be self-evident. Not only is it wearisome to walk around having to juggle the masks one needs to wear, but no one knows better than the actor that he or she is not the same as the character being played.

Conflict mounts between the role we are playing and what is real within us until the inevitable collapse onstage. In fact, there's really only one reason we ever "let loose" and outwardly express any negative emotion: it's because we can no longer maintain our role of being cool, calm, and in control. In other words, the mask has come off!

In today's world it is commonly accepted that social masks serve the purpose of the one who wears them. But this is not true, as evidenced by the pain in the lives of those who believe that putting on a loving or fearless face is the same as having realized those same qualities. The true purpose of any mask, whether that of others or our own, is to cover up the pain that hides behind it.

The first step in uncovering any lost treasure, whether that of sunken gold or to realize one's true purpose in life, is to remove the overburden, the accumulated debris that conceals it. Which brings us to this one last thought for those who hope to see the face of the immortal Self: it is spiritually impossible to hide and see at the same time.

KEY LESSON

It's impossible to separate being identified with some false purpose in life from the unconscious suffering that it produces.

Start Giving Yourself
What You Really Want

It's a little-known secret that our experience of life in any given moment is a direct reflection of what we actually value in that same moment. We may deny this unsettling truth, but when it comes to what we are in relationship with, inwardly and outwardly, actions speak louder than words—and, seen or not, all actions are a choice of one kind or another.

Nothing in the universe can make us choose to act against ourselves, as in when we consort with self-compromising negative states. Living in sorrow, with anger, or awash in regrets is a consensual affair. These dark states never dance alone; they must have a partner to produce their pain, which brings us to this good news: we are released from the dark embrace of any unhappy thought or feeling in the same moment we see that we've been tricked into dancing that troubled tango.

Use the following five insights to help you choose higher self-awareness as your new partner in life, and watch how effortless it becomes to start giving yourself what you really want.

- When you want peace within yourself more than you want to feel agitated over unwanted events taking place around you, then you will know the serenity for which you long.

- When you want to be at ease with yourself around friends and strangers alike more than you want that uneasy feeling that comes with fawning to win their approval, then you will know the quiet self-command for which you long.

- When you want to be patient with others more than you want to feel frustrated over

their inability to please you, then you will
know the forbearance for which you long.

- When you want authority over yourself
more than you want the conflict that
comes with trying to control others'
behavior, then you will know the
command for which you long.

- When you want to share in the fullness of
the present moment more than you want
the sinking feeling that you're missing out
on life, then you will know the unshakable
sense of wholeness for which you long.

KEY LESSON

*In this life there is no greater prize than one's
ability to be in full possession of oneself,
regardless of circumstance; neither is there
any task with so great a personal price.*

The Secret of Being
Successful in All Worlds

A reporter who had a deep and personal interest in higher spiritual matters heard of a certain teacher of truth who was held in high repute. But what caught the reporter's attention more than anything else was that this modern-day master was not only considered to have the Old Testament wisdom of a Solomon, but apparently he had Solomon's wealth as well.

Although the details were sketchy, word on the street held that, in his earlier years, he had been the successful CEO of an equally successful corporation that he had founded. Then, for reasons unknown, he retired and started his philanthropic and spiritual school around the same time. And so it came to pass that the reporter sought out an interview with this man of mystery, hoping to learn the secret of his success in both worlds.

Shortly thereafter, he was granted a personal audience with the master. "Thank you for allowing me this opportunity to speak with you personally. I won't take much of your time."

"Not a problem at all; how can I help you? What is it you would like to know?"

Something in the presence and manner of the master told him that there was little point in trying to mask his real reason for wanting to speak with him, so the reporter came right to the point.

"Sir, what I really want to know is how in the world you were able to amass such a fortune, not to mention become respected as being one of the wisest men on earth?"

The master gazed directly into the reporter's eyes. After many years of sitting with inquiring visitors of all levels, he could see easily into the hearts of those who had come to see him with such questions. What he found there determined how he answered them.

In this instance, he could see that the young man seated before him had sufficient self-knowledge to understand the subtlety of the answer he was about to give.

The master leaned forward and spoke: "In every sense of the word, the abundance in my life can all be attributed to a very simple method, something I started to practice when I was still a fairly young man. If you wish to know this secret, I would be glad to share it with you."

The reporter nodded yes.

The master continued his thought. "Every time I got ready to give someone my two cents, I learned to save them instead."

KEY LESSON

As to our course through life, whether we profit a little or a lot, do hold this one thought: we are made, each of us, as much by what we will as by what we will not.

Perfection Can't Be Possessed

Like a flower that emerges from rocky soil only on a fully moonlit night, truth appears—and its fragrance enriches whomever waits nearby. Then suddenly, just as it appears on no appointed schedule, it disappears again; only silence marks the empty spot from which it sprang.

Some try to dig it out but manage to extract only bits and pieces of petals, stem, and occasional root. But none can pull from the ground intact what is one with its nurturing soil, nor can any harm this precious flower they pursue, because it cannot be possessed; it is deathless.

Perhaps the harm in their pursuit, if any, is the almost impossible discovery that the beauty they so long to possess does not live apart from them; rather, *it lives for them*—even in those moments when they tear it apart, trying in vain to possess what it gives freely to those who die for the sight of it.

KEY LESSON

The highest and only lasting form of self-fulfillment is found through the completion of the moment itself and not in whatever one might try to extract and then capitalize on out of its appearance.

The Pain of My Father

Yesterday was my father's birthday; he passed away nearly two decades ago. Just realizing how much time has gone by since I last saw and spoke with him is a little shocking. He was a good man, loved by many, and with many loves that made his heart a full one.

There have been many times since he died that I've wished we could be together once more, but not for reasons one would easily guess, such as saying those things one wished had been spoken but weren't. For the most part, everything that could have been shared between us was said while he lived, and we spoke easily of our love for each other.

What was never shared, however, because I didn't know it at the time, was his pain.

It's a funny thing to think that you can live with someone, look at him daily, see all the signs of great personal suffering, and still not know anything at all about that person's pain. Only now can I see the real reasons for this kind of blindness.

No one can know the unspoken pain of another person until one knows his own. Only through this level of true self-knowledge does one unlock the secret of true compassion.

It's possible, I suppose, despite the birth of this higher self-understanding within me, that nothing would have changed between us—at least as far as how things appear between a father and a son sitting quietly together. But I do feel quite certain now that the many hours we did spend together would have been deeply enriched by the mutual awareness of our shared poverty, united by the pain that remained unspoken.

In some strange paradoxical way, to know one's own spiritual poverty is to see and know that same pain in everyone—and to value them all the more for it. And even more paradoxical is this fact: It's never too late to awaken to what is true, and to see how it changes all things present, future, and past.

KEY LESSON

True compassion is one and the same as one's conscious awareness that there is no separate self.

Remember Your Eternal Right to Be Free

The main reason we suffer or feel bad about ourselves or our current circumstances isn't because conditions in our lives have the power to punish us—because they don't. We suffer only from spiritual amnesia. We've forgotten that God, the Divine by whatever name you choose, is *Good*: not sometimes, not for just the "deserving," but for all...and in all ways.

Let's restate this last idea to see its rescuing wisdom from another angle: whenever we find ourselves identified with some dark stream of thoughts and feelings, as opposed to being quietly aware of their downward-trending presence, we fall—in that same moment—into a world filled with unwanted negative states. The reason so much of what's going on within and around us seems "bad" is because *that's all we can see.* Just as beauty is in the eye of the beholder, so it is true when it comes to all our inner states, including fear, depression, and bitterness. In such moments, having become bound up in thoughts and feelings we don't want, and then seeing a world that confirms our sense of captivity, we literally forget that *none of what we're going through is necessary.*

The only reason that we're standing in that storm of negative states is because *we've fallen asleep!* We've forgotten who we really are, including our divine right to call upon a power that instantly transports us out of harm's way. Anytime we can remember to do so, we are free to wake up and return to our true home—within us—beyond the reach of fear, doubt, or any other dark state.

If our wish is to walk freely through this world without fear of sudden storms—to know that we have an interior home whose light cannot be breached by any darkness—then our task is clear.

First, we must see how this spiritual amnesia blinds us and then binds us in a prison of false perceptions induced by having fallen spiritually asleep. To this end, use the following insight as the wake-up call to action that it is intended to be:

> *The freedom you have to let go and outgrow who you have been is not something created; it is and always will be yours, which means it cannot be destroyed any more than the onset of night destroys the light of the sun.*

Nothing in the universe can take from you your right to be spiritually free; it is a divine gift, which means that anytime you find yourself struggling to escape the grip of a negative state, it's only because you're in a dream from which you have yet to awaken. There's only one real prescription that has the power to end your pain: you must shake yourself awake from the forgetfulness that has caused you to forget your immortal Self.

KEY LESSON

Remembering the truth of yourself is one and the same as reclaiming your right to be free.

Walk Through Any Fearful Moment

We need never fear any quality or character that we see in ourselves. This isn't to say that such fears won't appear—they will, and they must as a result of our work to set ourselves free. After all, to walk out into the sunlight is to agree to see the shadows it makes. This brings us to a grand spiritual law that governs all things, including whatever we may presently fear:

Whatever we grow to understand about ourselves empowers us, accordingly, to stand over it.

For example, once we understand some tendency of ours that always gets us into trouble—like being argumentative, stubborn, or gullible—the temptation of that tendency no longer holds the authority over us that it once did. As our self-knowledge grows, so does the power we need to rise above the parts of ourselves that used to make us feel so powerless. Now we understand something of the real meaning behind the timeless teaching, "Know the truth, and the truth will set you free."

Here's another angle of this same great axiom: the only things we fear in this life are the unconscious projections of our own consciousness not yet awakened to itself. For instance, a young child is unable to understand that the dark shadow on his bedroom wall isn't a monster. *His feeling is real, but the "why" behind its appearance is a lie.* The mounting fear racing through his system is made substantial and validated by an unconscious resistance to what his own mind imagines is real in that same moment. The more he rejects what his mind projects on the screen of itself, the more real it becomes, so that not only is the child terrorized by the dark workings of his own imagination, but this same nature then tells him his choices, which are either to cry out or duck under the covers.

Regardless which way he goes, his guide is the very fear he tries to escape! Here's the key that opens the door to a whole new set of possibilities in the face of any fear:

Proceed while being afraid.

Forget all that nonsense about trying to appear brave, standing tall, or calling out for some rescuing force to chase away the shadow of what you fear. Such consoling images and ideals are the secret opposite of the very fears they are called on to reconcile. Here's everything you need to know in your moment of need: *what is true never fights with what is false*; it has no need to. Truth effortlessly dismisses any form of misunderstanding by the light of its own nature.

Within you dwells this very light of truth. Its unshakable courage in the face of any fear is because it knows that any darkness brought before it—no matter how large it may temporarily loom—will be effortlessly absorbed by it.

The substance and weight of any fearful shadow is only as great as what our imagination lends to it, which means it's not "this or that" fear we must have the courage to challenge. Rather, we must dare to prove to ourselves that any and all of our fearful conclusions are nothing more than an illusion. This is why the way out of any frightening, unwanted moment must be to go through it. After all, how else can we make the liberating discovery that our fears are just shadows without substance? Only by this action will we know the truth that frees us from fear...because only by its light can we see that we've never had anything real to fear.

KEY LESSON

In the end, nothing we can win in this life can enrich us half as much as what we are willing to lose for the sake of living without fear.

You Are Created to Change

We all have those moments when life rears up, when it seems certain that we're about to be trampled by forces greater than ourselves! But regardless of how you may feel in the face of any given challenge, you may rest assured of the following fact: you are created to outgrow any temporary limitation this challenge serves to reveal to you about yourself... no matter how difficult the task may seem to be.

Yes, you may be unprepared at its outset, just as each year a bare tree can't know in advance the weight of a heavy winter snowfall until its branches bend and maybe even break beneath it. But no tree is its limbs, and neither are you made less for what you can't do or carry when first challenged by something that seems too great for you to handle.

Learn to trust the following spiritual fact by daring to prove it to yourself as many times as it takes until you are free of fear: whatever may be your present weakness, it is only temporary—providing you're willing to persist, *to wade into what seems greater than you are*, and then test this truth time and time again.

The unimaginable reward of persisting through whatever stands in your way is the eventual and inevitable discovery that *you are created to change*.

KEY LESSON

*Since the nature of real life is genesis itself—
the ceaseless rebirth of "what has been" giving
way to "what is and will be"—this alone tells
you that you have the power to change.*

The Power to
Change Your Past

So many people today are bitter, broken-hearted, or just plain angry because of what happened to them while growing up. The reasons for their resentment or regret are as countless as are the number of unconscious people who unknowingly create such pain in the lives of those they hurt. But nothing that happened yesterday—as horrendous as it may have been—has authority over the present moment and its new possibilities.

We may sense the truth of this spiritual fact but have been unable to put its power to work in our life. Here's what to do whenever we find ourselves wrapped in the flames of that burning house called our painful past:

Get out of it!

Here's the "how" part, although each of us must see the following truths that help free us from ourselves.

The true present moment cannot burn anything, let alone your immortal Self; it is the strange allure of reliving the past that punishes those unwary enough to wander back through it, searching for some resolution that can't be found there.

Any sorrow, resentment, or anxiety brought over and into the living now can only be an echo of some event now past. Try to see this liberating fact: no pain from the past can make itself present unless the mind, asleep to itself, is deceived into revisiting the painful memory of that misery.

Nevertheless, in the same moment this negative image (replete with dark emotions) is recollected, *it is resisted by the same sleeping mind that resurrected it!* This reaction makes the unwary a victim of nothing other than having sleepwalked into the stored memories of his or her own unwanted past, and though the pain is real, no doubt, it is a pain born of resisting a dream whose dark content creates misery for anyone caught in its realm. This brings us to a key idea for those who wish to leave a conflicted past behind:

Who you really are—your immortal Self—doesn't live in the past, and therefore cannot be punished by anything that happened there.

If anything, the repeated pain of reliving whatever the problems may have been should show us that we've arrived in the wrong place, led there by misguided parts of us.

Imagine sleepwalking into a rundown, dangerous neighborhood and suddenly awakening to your situation. There's no doubt as to your next action: you would get out of that place as fast as you could. Wisdom, if not pure instinct, prevails, and the same intelligence should hold true for us when it comes to our spiritual lives. What "once was" lives on only in an unconscious "neighborhood" in ourselves—one where we no longer belong. This in-the-dark level of consciousness is populated with the shadows of former painful experiences, both real and imagined. But their power over us runs only as deep as we are identified with that dream world into which we have fallen. We walk out of there by waking up, or by bringing our attention back into the presence of the living moment, where it belongs.

No one can teach us to leave the world of what was or to abandon those unconscious parts of us that actually need to relive their pain in order to live on; they cannot see themselves for what they are, nor do they want to.

We must see them, their world, and the pain of their reality as being something we no longer wish to walk with or through. Nothing can delay our departure from this lower level of self, any more than the ground floor of a skyscraper can keep you from taking its elevator all the way up to the observation deck.

You cannot do the work of starting life over and be busy reliving your past at the same time. Being new is a deliberate choice: it is an act of alignment that places you in conscious contact with a living presence that's incapable of repeating itself.

Stop Complaining and Start Changing

Two construction workers, employed on the same high-rise job for many months now, are seated on a steel beam overlooking the city. It's time for lunch and a little relaxation from the stress of the day. But every day since they first started taking their meal together, one of the men, Dave, has never failed to voice some complaint about his sandwich, saying things like "Oh no, not meatloaf again" or "Dang, this bread is hard as a rock!"

One afternoon, as Dave starts up his usual negative review of his sandwich, slamming one thing or another about its contents or how it's been "thrown together," his coworker, Ben, just doesn't want to hear it anymore. And so, collecting himself carefully so as not to tread on Dave's toes, he speaks up.

"Look, Dave—granted, I don't know much about your life at home, and I don't mean to stick my nose where it doesn't belong—but why not ask your wife to make you something different? I'm sure she wouldn't mind."

"No," says Dave, "it's not my wife's fault. Tammy's the greatest—a saint, really. She works the late-night shift at the hospital as a nurse." And then, after taking a hard look at the sandwich in his hand, he finishes his thought. "As a rule, she hardly ever gets back home before I leave for work."

"Hmmm," says Ben, pausing to think things through for a moment. "Then I guess I don't understand…"

"What's that?" asks Dave.

Ben continues: "Well, who makes your sandwich for you each morning?"

With that, Dave looks him straight in the eye, as if the answer is too obvious to miss. "Who do you think makes it? *I do!*"

Most people would rather complain about some painful life pattern than dare to meet the level of their own consciousness responsible for its repeated appearance ... and therein do the work needed to change it once and for all.

Ten Ways to Stop Feeling Sorry for Yourself

Here is a heart-healing, sadness-ending spiritual fact. Welcome the light it brings by being willing to see the truth hidden within it:

Regardless of how disappointing or painful it may have been, nothing real lives in your past that can grab you and make you its captive any more than a dark shadow has the power to keep you from walking into the sunlight.

Now, add to this fact the realization that there is never a good reason to go along with feeling bad about yourself, and you're on your way to living in a world without self-pity.

To help speed your journey, welcome the ten special insights that follow as your trusted guides to a life free of tears. The more you work inwardly to understand their wisdom, the freer you will find yourself of all dark, self-compromising states.

- The only thing self-pity accomplishes is that it makes your life worse.

- No matter how you look at it, not wanting some negative emotional state doesn't separate you from what is unwanted; it binds you to it!

- Being wrapped up in self-pity completely spoils any chance of being able to see new possibilities as they appear; besides, no one likes sour milk.

- The only thing that grows from cultivating any dark seed of sorrow is more bitter fruit.

- Manipulating others to feel sorry for you is like an alcoholic asking for a gift certificate to a liquor store.

- Self-pity is the campsite of self-defeat; it is a dark refuge for those parts of us that would rather wallow in what cannot be than dare to explore what is possible.

- Feeling sorry for yourself is a slow-acting poison; it first corrupts and then consumes the heart, choking it with dark, useless emotions.

- You cannot separate the reasons you have for feeling sorry for yourself from the sorry way you feel.

- The heart watered by tears of self-pity soon turns to stone; it is incapable of compassion.

- Agreeing to live with sad regrets only ensures they'll still be with you tomorrow.

KEY LESSON

*There is no greater unnecessary limitation
in this life—replete with all its sorrow—than
one's unseen agreement to live in and with
the bittersweet bliss of self-ignorance.*

Discover Your Unseen
Attachment to Heartache

When it comes to healing mental or emotional pain, the first step to freeing oneself is in seeing the following facts: resistance to anything (including psychological pain) is a secret form of fascination with it, and to be fascinated with anything—regardless of its nature—is to be identified with it.

Add to these insights the fact that to be identified with something is to be attached to the same, and then one can see how an unseen dependency on dark states gets formed.

It is the light of this understanding alone that shatters not just the walls of one's psychological prison, but also the level of "self" that has built and maintained them. Therefore, it is an axiom: *before one can be healed, one must stop hurting oneself.* There is no other way.

KEY LESSON

All attachments are secret heartaches disguised as lovers.

Use Unwanted Moments
to Set You Free

My little house sits on a mountain in southern Oregon and is surrounded on all sides by a natural preserve. The wildlife there is as varied as it is abundant, but it mostly consists of the kind of creatures one sees in Bambi movies. Now, let me set the stage for this short lesson in letting go.

It was late in the afternoon by the time I had finished. My preparations had been impeccable. After a long series of skirmishes—with more losses than victories—it looked as if the situation had been contained; every possible contingency had been considered.

Spread out before me—arrayed and displayed like giant Christmas ornaments hanging from various trees—was my collection of bird feeders. Most hung from branches, a couple were on poles, and there was a single long cylindrical-shaped one whose base would spin if something heavier than a bird was to sit or pull upon it. Red plastic cones were suspended over a few hanging feeders, while the others were enmeshed in wire with hand-cut, calculated openings allowing nothing larger than a Steller's jay to enter its hallowed feeding area.

As I stood there on my outdoor deck surveying the feeders, a wave of satisfaction passed over and through me. *Come on!* I thought to myself, issuing a silent challenge to the gang of tree squirrels that I had seen pillaging my feeders since day one. Had I gone too far? No! In truth, I couldn't wait for the first wave of these four-legged monkeys to hit the beachhead I had prepared just for them. But I would have wait: the sun was setting, and experience had shown that most of them liked to come a little after eight AM. So I retired from my observation post, waiting for the next day with more than a little excitement.

Awakening the next morning, I couldn't wait to see how things would unfold. To date, even my best invention to thwart these squirrels had not only failed, but before too long, they had turned it into their personal gymnasium. *Not today! It belonged to me.* At least that's what I thought until I looked outside at my yard. There is no way in heaven anyone could have anticipated the carnage.

My hanging feeders were all torn down, smashed to pieces. Both of the metal poles that housed the platform feeders were bent over to the ground, twisted like straws. Shards were all that was left of the birdhouses. I was stunned beyond belief. My mind raced as I ran outside to survey the damages; what could have done this? Had the gods sent a super squirrel to wreak havoc—to seek revenge on me for wanting to balance the scale of nature?

A moment later, all was clear; I could see the whole story. Ah, yes; yet another lesson in letting go of the best-laid plans. The laugh was on me. After all, nothing like this had ever happened before.

Who could have anticipated an overnight visit from a hungry bear?

KEY LESSON

The unwanted moments in our life do not come as some blind force set against our best interests; rather, they come to help us realize what our best interests actually are.

Be Lifted Into the World of the Divine

There is one essential reason why there is so much constant heartache and war on this earth, and why conflict has continued as it has down through the ages. The answer may surprise you. We do not understand the nature of our own pain—our suffering. Billions of us live with almost no understanding of how much hurt lies hidden in our hearts and minds; in this case, ignorance is *not* bliss.

In fact, most of us carry, buried in the depths of ourselves, untold amounts of unconscious woe. Regardless of our religion, skin color, social position, or cultural conditioning, psychological pain plays no favorites; we all pay the price of the ensuing blame game.

From battles with family and friends, all the way up to world conflict, wars persist because the pain that drives this great divide between us is not understood; in the end, it is the ignorance of this pain that manifests war. So, even though it isn't exactly a popular study, we must examine our suffering. It is a law: *what remains concealed can never be healed*. Only true self-knowledge can bring an end to our tears, whatever their nature. In the end, the only way out of any "rain of pain" is to wake up and walk away from the self-ignorance from out of which it pours. Use the following new self-knowledge to help you step into the sunlight of your true self.

Everything created is brought into existence through the marriage of opposites; birth takes place in the womb of opposing forces. And, though it seems a paradox, the inevitable destruction, or undoing of any creation, is also the play of opposing forces.

These last few ideas express one of the laws of thermodynamics: namely, that energy can neither be created nor destroyed, only change its form.

Creation is the "play" of these eternal energies, represented in the West by the Father, Son, and Holy Spirit and in the East by Brahma, Vishnu, and Shiva, each a trinity of divinity; the invisible source of love, light, life, and death, as well as the laws overseeing their relationships. Not only do these eternal laws create and govern the universe in which we live, their tireless work is exactly the same within us. As we're about to see, self-liberation is directly proportionate to our ability to understand the ceaseless interplay of these timeless forces.

Wherever there is opposition, resistance follows. For instance, in nature, in the physical world, this kind of conflict is natural, necessary, and accepted. After the winds pass, the trees they've touched—having been exercised and duly strengthened, accordingly—resume their natural course of life. They don't stand there and resent the wind that stirred them up and perhaps even stripped them of their beautiful leaves. This interaction between what is active (the wind) and what is passive (the tree) sees to the gradual perfection of everything created—or at least it's intended to.

Whenever we experience unwanted moments, or "winds" that challenge both our vessel and our vision of some safe harbor to come, we resist them tooth and nail. We fight with almost anything or anyone who seems to oppose us, struggling in vain to control or avoid what we see as punishing us. And for this opposition we reap its result: the unconscious pain of being in conflict with life's higher purposes.

What we fail to realize, however, is that without those opposing forces working their way in and upon us, inertia would rule the day: our nature would be unable to change. Strange as it seems, without consciously realizing our own limitations, it's impossible for our understanding to grow; and, without higher self-awareness, we could never come to this next vital realization:

What we now perceive as painful or opposing conditions in life are secretly complementary opposites. They don't just complete one another, they serve to perfect all of creation through each complete cycle of life and death that they help birth.

In other words, without them nothing new can be conceived. Rebirth is made possible because something dies to ensure it. In this eternal law of life hides a new understanding, a great key that many have sought but only few have ever found. As we are about to see, it opens an interior door that leads directly to a conscious relationship with the divinity within us.

Life will always give you something greater than what it's asked you for, providing you're willing to let go of that part of yourself that, for fear of the new, favors what's old. It's impossible to cling to who you have been ... and be free of yourself at the same time.

This great exchange and the self-sacrifice for which it calls is the spiritual secret of secrets. Your willingness to enact it is the same as finding the "perfect love that casts out all fears."

Your success depends upon being able to see that real life is secretly a single, beautiful movement incapable of contradicting itself. The more you understand how this one truth includes *everything that happens to you,* the more you'll be willing to let go and enter into the flow of even your most unwanted moments!

In this light, the old adage "let go and let God" takes on a whole new meaning; it is a single action born of two harmonizing parts: the need to release yourself from a part of yourself that no longer serves your best interests, and the simultaneous rebirth of a new order of self beyond anything you could have imagined.

KEY LESSON

Fearlessness comes with the birth of this new understanding: the only reason life changes as it does is to reveal the secret goodness underlying those same changes.

Shatter the Bonds of False Beliefs and Be Free

Near the end of a busy afternoon, a senior caddie at an exclusive golf club was making his appointed rounds—double-checking that everything was in its proper place—when he entered the clubhouse locker room. Much to his shock, he saw an obviously completely exhausted man spread-eagled on the floor.

A moment later, he recognized the man as a fairly new member of the club. At first he feared the man may have fallen and hit his head, but after touching him gently, the man leaped to his feet, a terrified look in his eye.

"Are you all right?" asked the caddie. "You gave me a start, finding you lying there like that."

"Yes... sorry, really... yes... I'm okay," answered the man.

"Are you sure? You look completely drained. If you don't mind me asking, how many rounds of golf did you play today? Never saw a man so tired as to pass out on the floor!"

Hesitating a bit, the member replied, "Well, truthfully, I haven't been out to play yet."

Squinting his eyes, trying to fathom what the man had said, the caddie asked, "I'm not sure I understand, then. You look as if you'd played seventy-two holes."

The man's face turned slightly red, obviously embarrassed over something, and then he answered, barely above a whisper, "I guess I was so worried about making a good impression—what with being new here and all—that while I was getting dressed to play, I had so many fearful thoughts about my swing, I must have worn myself out!"

The caddie just smiled, knowing exactly what the man had just put himself through. He understood just how easy it was to bury oneself under the weight of false beliefs and the equally false set of responsibilities that come with them.

In this instance, to believe that we're only as worthwhile as others agree to see us burdens us with feeling that winning the good opinion of others is somehow our responsibility. Such a mistaken mindset leaves us the perennial victim of our relationships and never the victor in them.

The only way we can be released from any painful sense of false responsibility is to see that it is based in a false belief. To see through the false belief is to be released from the weight of useless false responsibilities.

Study carefully the following list of six false beliefs and the false responsibilities that are never far away from them. Dare to learn everything you can about your own false beliefs, then watch how the weight of false responsibilities falls off of you.

False Belief #1: Unwanted moments are to be avoided at all costs.

False Responsibility: You feel as if you must remain in control of everyone and everything at all times.

True Responsibility: Welcome everything that happens to you as an opportunity to see through and transcend the unconscious burden of being someone laden with any false beliefs.

False Belief #2: You are only as valuable or worthless as other people agree that you are.

False Responsibility: You're convinced that you must do whatever it takes to win the approval of everyone you meet.

True Responsibility: Be real. Learn what it means to be in possession of yourself, starting with reclaiming your life.

False Belief #3: You are responsible for the happiness or unhappiness that others feel.

False Responsibility: You must always compromise yourself to ensure the contentment of everyone else.

True Responsibility: Stay out of the lives of all those who expect you to do for them what they won't do for themselves.

False Belief #4: You must learn to tolerate friends and family who have agreed to live with and justify negative states.

False Responsibility: You must constantly smooth over rocky situations, ensuring that no one rocks anyone's boat enough to tip it over.

True Responsibility: See all negative states as the unconscious, dark emotions that they are, and refuse to justify them in yourself or anyone else.

False Belief #5: You can change what happened yesterday by revisiting and reliving it today.

False Responsibility: Unless you worry about and suffer over your past, your tomorrows are not going to turn out right.

True Responsibility: You can be a new person right now. Let go of anything that wants to revisit and relive the past.

False Belief #6: Feeling deeply stressed proves you really care about whatever you're suffering over.

False Responsibility: It's up to you to shoulder the weight of those painful thoughts and feelings that want to drag you down.

True Responsibility: See that agreeing to suffer from your own mental and emotional states makes as much sense as blaming the French fry that just burned your mouth.

I encourage you to sit down and make your own list of false beliefs and the legion of false responsibilities that come with them. Remember that your one true responsibility in life—the one action that will always see to your success in life—is to always be as awake and receptive to the present moment as you can be.

If we refuse to see what life is trying to show us about ourselves, then we can't learn. If we don't learn the truth of ourselves, then true self-knowledge becomes impossible. Without higher self-knowledge, there is no way to rise above ourselves and reach that innermost path that alone leads to the fulfillment of our highest possibilities.

The real, unseen cause of our fear is the false belief that life can throw something—anything— at us that's greater than our ability to change it. But this is simply not true. No matter what our culture, tradition, or religious background, within each of us lives a fearless immortal Self: a transcendent nature that never fears unforeseen changes in life any more than the sun trembles before the temporary appearance of some shadow cast by its own light.

The Three Stages
of Self-Realization

The pitfalls along the upper path leading to the realization of the immortal Self are well marked by the aspiring souls who have gone before us. Their legacy of spiritual insights and revelations serves as signposts along the way for all who wish to awaken their sleeping divinity.

In this instance, all traditions in the East and West point out three distinct stages of realization through which the aspirant must pass. Each stage is unique in its character, and none may be skipped; much like a seed gives rise to a flower and from that flower is born its fruit, all three stages are required or nothing real can grow.

Stage one: When first stumbling upon the true upper path, most aspiring souls are highly motivated; they share a single positive sentiment: "Watch out, world, I'm coming through! *Nothing* is impossible for me." This stage is called false certainty.

The newly fledged seeker cannot yet see that his or her budding confidence is the byproduct of self-flattering images and their attending pleasures; the aspirant is fully identified with the promise of imagined powers just ahead. Filled with the sensation of standing in this false light, success feels certain. It only seems logical to think, "Very soon now, whatever I wish to manifest shall come to pass; money, power, and people will be mine to use as I please. And, as soon as God acknowledges my greatness, everyone else will, as well. No one and nothing will ever stand in my way again." This is the first stage.

Stage two is marked by an ever-increasing sense of doubt. This is the stage of uncertainty. Many of the earlier illusions have been crushed, and even small successes have proven themselves to be painfully incomplete. What was once believed to be strength or resilience—their best qualities—show themselves as being either unavailable when needed most or, worse, nonexistent. The aspirant enters into a dark place; none of his or her imagined powers have any real light to offer. It seems like there is no way out of the darkness.

So the aspirant now thinks, "This path—my life—is impossible! Virtually nothing I've done to awaken has changed anything, save for showing me how asleep I am!" Now the aspirant feels lost, like a ship adrift at sea with holes in its hull! Slowly a conviction grows that either the Divine has abandoned him or that her whole journey was never anything but a spiritual pipe dream; it's at this point that the aspirant enters into the "dark night of the soul"...which, if walked through, brings them to the third stage of their journey.

Stage three: If we go through the first stage of ego-induced dreams born of what amounts to an imagined divinity—where all seems possible—and then stay the course through the next necessary stage of ego-shattering shocks—where all seems impossible because we now imagine ourselves to be the lowest creature on earth—*then* we reach the third stage.

Here we gradually come to realize that both our former "great" self and our "terrible" self are secretly one nature, a level of consciousness that sleeps in a world of its own dreams. In the light of this revelation—that these two seemingly separate selves are secretly one—we come to a divine realization:

Who we really are, our true self, is *neither one of these false identities*. The whole illusion collapses before our interior eyes. We are moved effortlessly from a world of dreams—ruled by illusions—into the reality of a conscious relationship with our immortal Self.

The three stages are complete. We realize their culmination and receive their divine gift of *real certainty*.

KEY LESSON

The false self, ever pursuing or struggling to protect the dream of its imagined sense of importance, doesn't care how it sabotages itself or victimizes others. All that matters to this divided self is that it find a way to validate its pressing need to feel significant, which means its character is incapable of humility, compassion, or remorse. It loves itself and itself only.

The True Nature of Self-Respect

True respect for oneself must include the presence of a humility that tempers the temptation inherent in all forms of self-evaluation; otherwise, what we call respect for ourselves is really just a form of secret self-admiration: a false, fearful state that has as much in common with real self-respect as does a postcard picture of a rugged coastline with the towering cliffs and surging waves that it depicts.

To see the truth of this, consider the deep respect we may feel towards those others whom we know have gone before us, daring what they must to become the instrument of something divine, whatever their chosen endeavor.

We know and sense without having to think about it that these individuals have attained a relationship with something greater, wiser, than we have. There is a natural respect for anyone who has transcended their limitations and, for this sacrifice, has ascended to realize a wisdom, compassion, capacity, or contentment that surpasses our own. And in this reverence we find a true sense of humility that moves us in two ways—but in one direction.

First comes the recognition of a quality, character, patience, or skill greater than anything we have yet known; and, at the same time, the tangible presence of such a possibility beckons us upward and onward so that we aspire to reach and realize those same heights, if not higher. Of course, some form of painful comparison may try to corrupt this newly awakened need. But, fortunately for us, any real spiritual need is protected by the same intelligence that seeds it in us. In this case, the gravity of our gratitude outweighs these petty concerns. After all, who in his or her right mind resents a towering mountain peak because it radiates a timeless majesty? The wise wish, naturally, to gain this viewpoint whatever the cost, which leads us to this last revelation:

True respect for oneself is the realization of one's immortal Self; it never can be won any more than one can win the innocence of a child. It is an awakening, a simultaneous glimpse of one's low estate from on high; as such, it includes the quiet humility born of seeing, at once, our highest possibilities and the present level of self that stands beneath them, looking up at them.

KEY LESSON

Awakening to realize that whatever you judge in another is only what you've yet to see in yourself is the beginning of true humility; it is the first step toward a new and higher order of compassion.

Learn to Relax with Others
by Releasing Yourself

Here's a simple but ultimately very self-liberating action to take if you wish to reduce
the amount of stress and anxiety that you
feel in the company of others, friends, or family:

*Choose to be more interested in quietly discovering
the truth of yourself than you are in trying to prove
yourself as being somehow special or otherwise
infallible.*

Within each of us dwells a certain lower level of
"self" whose chief feature is to ensure that no one
ever doubts its perfection. Whenever we identify with

this unconscious nature, we embody its fear—a condition that only proves, by the way, its imperfection.

Besides, who wants to protect what is inherently blind to itself even as it insists upon its 20/20 vision?

KEY LESSON

It's always the right time to discover something new and true about your own nature, even if, in that moment, what you've uncovered seems altogether wrong.

Slay the Dragon
of Painful Desire

As their limousine pulled up in front of the massive columns leading into the Institute for a Better Planet, Paul looked over at the face of his best friend, Bret, to try and get a bead on what he must be feeling. After all, it wasn't every day that a man received the Institute's most coveted Humanitarian Award, let alone be honored by the dozens of dignitaries who had turned out for the evening's grand event.

But if Bret was excited, there was no sign of it; in fact, he seemed calm, collected, and as if he was completely comfortable with all the fuss being made over his appearance.

Paul felt proud to share in Bret's moment and could hardly keep himself from smiling over his old friend's good fortune. Stepping out of the limo, the two of them were greeted by the clicking sound of fifty cameras mixed in with the polite applause of people standing by who must have been waiting for their arrival. In what seemed like less than a moment later, someone from the Institute rushed into the throng to rescue them, sweeping them off to the great hall, where most of the guests were already waiting.

Paul had never seen anything quite like it: row upon row of fabulous buffet tables filled with fantastic ice sculptures standing over mountains of jumbo shrimp and lobster tails. Table after table, there were bubbling champagne towers, piles of king crab legs, and platters filled with delicate meats and fine cheeses, all interspaced with the most colorful and wonderful display of fresh vegetables and exotic fruits one could imagine. He was overwhelmed at the opulence of food and drink; actually, he was decidedly shocked at the extravagance. *Surely,* he thought to himself, *there had to be better ways to spend the precious funds donated to the Institute*, but what could he say to anyone that wouldn't sour the moment?

Shaking off the weight of his own thoughts, he turned to see how Bret was faring, expecting to see a big smile on his face. But what he saw was nothing like that; in fact, he was shocked to see Bret glaring at a table centerpiece that was a virtual cornucopia of fresh vegetables and creamy-looking dips. His negative state was almost tangible; something had overtaken him completely. *What on earth?* Paul thought to himself. He slipped as close to Bret as he could, to speak with him so no one else could hear.

"Snap out of it, man!" he said in somewhat urgent but friendly tones. "What's with you? This whole affair is in *your* honor, and you look like someone just stole your Christmas stocking!"

Bret turned and stared at Paul for a moment, and then said, "Can you believe it? Just *look* at that..." and then he turned his burning gaze back at the center of the table before them. "What's wrong with these people? What were they thinking?"

Paul could see that Bret was referring to something on the table, but it made no sense at all. So he asked again, "What are you so unhappy about that you would let it ruin this perfect evening?" But no answer came—just a stony silence as Bret continued glaring at something on the buffet table.

"Bret!" Paul said. "I'm talking to *you*—what's wrong? Tell me, and I'll do whatever I can to fix it."

Bret slowly turned to face his friend and, lifting his arm, pointed with his index finger to the centerpiece of the table. It was a perfect model of the earth shaped out of fresh vegetables, with a bright red heart made of perfect cherry tomatoes.

"*Look!*" The word seethed out of Bret's mouth. "Look at that! You want to know what's wrong? *That's* what's wrong!"

Paul craned his head from side to side, trying to see what Bret was pointing to, but he could see nothing save the beautiful arrangement of fresh food. "I don't see anything wrong, Bret," said Paul. "What are you looking at that I don't see?"

Bret continued on with his rant as if it made perfect sense. "*Everyone* knows I can't stand cherry tomatoes, and yet"—pointing his finger again to the heart of the display—"*there must be a thousand of them, right there in the center of everything. The night is ruined!*"

For many of us, such a story seems implausible; on the surface, it makes no sense. After all, how can someone be given so much and—rather than being grateful for the abundance of these gifts—be so negative over a single element in the midst of them? But closer examination of this situation, and the inconsolable level of self that gives rise to it, may show us that we have more in common with this discontented character than not.

Maybe we've never had a party thrown in our honor, but surely we've known similar "perfect" moments in our lives. Who hasn't been in the middle of a dream vacation, without a care in the world, when—*kaboom!* In spite of the abundance around us, we're suddenly negative, deeply distressed simply because something or someone fails to please us according to our expectations!

Or how about those moments when—regardless of how many of our friends may hold us in high esteem—a single disapproving face, even from a stranger, obliterates our sense of self-worth? In an instant we feel ourselves all alone, unloved, stripped of value.

As difficult and shocking as it may be to consider, the experiences noted above make the following fact irrefutable: within us dwells a certain level of unconscious desire that loves to *not want*. It has but one purpose: this part of us "lives" to resist anything that doesn't live up to its expectations. Why would anything want to live like that? Because what this dark nature likes most of all is *being negative*!

In truth, most of us know very little about this negative side of desire because each time it rises up to reject something, we're inwardly directed to look at what it blames for our pain. And by this misdirection we're blinded to the fact that this nature is, in and of itself, the source of the discontentment we're given to feel.

Now, contrast this nature to the more familiar and "friendly" side of desire that we all know and embrace: it "lives" to *want*; this is a feeling we all know quite well, including the fact that if not momentarily content in the embrace of something it "loves"—this nature is already looking around for what's next. We accept, even lionize this level of self that exists to pursue and to possess what it imagines will make it feel whole and happy. After all, it seems harmless enough to want what we want and to give ourselves freely to this warm and fuzzy side of our desires. But, taking all of these facts above in hand, we can see what few before us have had eyes to see:

Desire is a coin with two faces. One side is known and embraced freely, its appearance welcomed for the pleasures it promises. However, the flip side of this coin, its unseen face, belongs to Desire's dark twin who—being the opposite of her sister—lives only *to resist*. This nature, the essence of denial itself, conceals its painful presence within us by speaking to us in our own voice, telling us why we feel discontent even as it whispers to us the reasons why we must suffer accordingly.

Let's summarize these discoveries and welcome their revelations, even if they may point to something momentarily disconcerting. It's impossible for us to identify with the pleasure of wanting something without encountering the pain of *not wanting* whatever will come to stand between that desire and its fulfillment. In other words, on the flip side of that invigorating feeling called "Yes, I want (this)" is that debilitating state called, "No! I don't want (that)."

Personal experience validates this finding. No matter what we give to desire, *it's never enough.* One way or another, by its very nature, *desire always wants more*... which leads us to this next astonishing revelation. Please take your time to ponder its meaning until you can see the many self-liberating truths hidden within it.

> *Our inevitable sense of dissatisfaction with life is inseparable from whatever desire sends us out to claim in the name of its imagined contentment to come.*

The nature of desire can never know lasting contentment because it is literally set against itself; it is a "house divided" in the truest sense of the words, and it only stands for as long as it can keep us shoring up its constantly collapsing sides.

Learning to welcome and then act from this new self-knowledge is the same as embracing a new order of consciousness that can't be tricked into acting against itself.

KEY LESSON

Since no desire can complete itself by itself through anything it imagines, its only recourse is to imagine more of whatever failed to satisfy it the first time around. This unseen cycle is the mainspring of addiction, among other unseen self-compromising states, and it drives that dark engine called greed, as unconscious desire keeps trying to fill a bucket with no bottom by pouring imaginary water into it.

Drop Painful Demands

In moments of challenge, the tendency is to resist the unwanted situation because of the pain that seems to appear with it. But the truth behind these moments is very different from our habitual perception and mechanical reaction to them.

No moment in and of itself causes our pain. The real source of our suffering is some unconscious demand that we've placed on life…and not what life seems to be denying us.

We can't change others—or the purpose of any given moment as it unfolds—but we can work to place one less demand upon both. Only in this action can we hope to find the freedom for which we seek, because the only thing that imprisons us, in the end, is our resistance to whatever runs against our deeply seated demands.

KEY LESSON

The pain of impatience, anxiety, or most any stressed state doesn't exist without some unseen level of ourselves secretly demanding that events unfold precisely as we've imagined them.

Resistance Is Negative
Attraction

Tucked into a deep, high remote canyon somewhere in the Himalayan Mountains sits a secret monastery assigned the task of training
would-be adepts in the lost science of self-realization.
Only those who have studied there or who are allowed to live there even know it exists.

Early one morning, after a particularly difficult
meditation period following weeks of futile attempts
to quiet his mind, one of the young aspirants rush-
es over and throws himself at the feet of the senior
monk, crying, pleading, "Master, please help! I feel as

if I have come to a complete dead end in my work to be free. No matter what I do, there's no escape."

The master pulled the young monk up from off of the ground, looked quietly into his tear-filled eyes, and then began speaking in a stern but gentle voice. "First, young one, wake up; drop these useless dramatics. Only then can we hope to learn something together."

Using the sleeve on the arm of his robe to wipe his face, the aspirant did the best he could to sober himself, and said, "Yes, of course, Master: as you wish."

"Now then," said the Master. "What is it that you want to ask of me?"

The aspirant gathered himself together and said in a quiet voice, "Master, what's wrong with me? I can't shake off these negative states! Why do they keep coming back to me no matter what I do to get rid of them?"

The Master paused and answered, "Because you don't want them."

Resistance to unwanted moments seems intelligent; it feels wise to disagree with whatever we perceive as punishing. But this resistance does not separate us from our suffering; instead, it binds us to it.

*Five Simple Laws to Help You Reach
Your Highest Spiritual Possibilities*

We are all familiar with the general laws that govern our physical well-being: eat healthy foods, exercise both mind and body, and avoid toxic people and places whenever possible. Adhere to these simple laws and be relatively free from suffering; break them, and you place yourself under another set of laws that pretty much guarantee you won't be happy with how you feel.

Much in the same way, as shown above, there are spiritual laws that govern what we will or won't discover about ourselves in this lifetime. And when we understand that self-knowledge is to our spiritual growth what a spring rain is to the wildflower seeds that await it, then we also realize how vital it is to not just embrace these higher laws but embrace them mind, body, and soul.

Following are five laws to help you awaken and realize your highest spiritual possibilities.

If It Doesn't Flow, There's More to Know

Learn to recognize all forms of strain—whether at work, in your creative efforts, or in your relationships—as being unnecessary. The mounting friction you feel when busy at some labor is never caused by the task at hand but by what you don't yet know about it. This means the only real reason for your strain is that you've got hold of a wrong idea you don't yet see as wrong. This new insight allows you to release yourself by showing you what you need to know. Flowing follows your new knowing.

Refuse to Take the Easy Way

There's no getting away from what you don't know, which is why anytime you feel compelled to go around a problem by taking the easy way, i.e., pretending it doesn't exist, blaming others for your pain, or meeting it with half-measures, that problem always comes back around again. And isn't that what makes life seem so hard? Learn to see the "easy way" as a lying thought that keeps you tied up and doing hard time. Getting through something is not the same as having it completed. And as this insight grows, so will your understanding that the whole idea of the "hard way" has always been just a lying thought as well. Now you know: the complete way is the easy way. So volunteer to make the "hard way" your way, and learn what it means to live the effortless way.

Watch for the Opportunity to Learn Something New

Everything is changing all the time. That means life is an endless occasion for learning something new—but this means more than meets the eye. Just as you're a part of everything, everything is a part of you. The whole of life is connected. And your ability to learn is part of the wonder of this complete but ever-changing whole. Learning serves as a window into the complex world you see around you, and through it you may also look into the "you" that's busy looking into the world. And when you've learned there's no end to what you can see about the amazing worlds spinning both around and within you, you'll also know there's no end to you. So stay awake, and learn something new every day. You'll love how that makes you feel about yourself.

See Conclusions as Limitations

If you approach the possibilities of learning about your life as being limitless—which they are—then it follows that any conclusion you reach about yourself has to be an unseen limitation. Why? *Because there's always more to see.* For instance, let yourself see that all conclusions are illusions when it comes to the security they promise. There may be security in a prison, but there are also no choices behind its confining walls. Learn to see all conclusions about yourself as invisible cells, for that's exactly what they are. The seeming security these conclusions offer is a poor substitute for the real security of knowing that who you really are is always free to be something higher.

Persistence Always Prevails

If you'll persist with your sincere wish for higher learning, you can't help but succeed. Persistence always prevails because part of its power is to hold you in place until either the world lines up with your wish or you see that your wish is out of line. But, for whichever way it turns in that moment, you've won something that only persistence can buy. If you get what you *think* you have to have to be happy and you're still not satisfied, then *you've learned what doesn't work*. Now you can go on to higher things. And should you learn you've been wearing yourself out with useless wishes, then this discovery allows you to turn your energies in a new direction: self-liberation.

KEY LESSON

*Allowing yourself to act in such a way
as to deny yourself a new awareness of
yourself—whatever its quality—is the same
as refusing your right to realize the limitless
depth and breadth of the immortal Self.*

Growing Into a Love That Lasts

Here is a simple set of instructions for those who want their love to last:

Don't try to please each other, for each of you has constantly changing pleasures. Instead, strive to please love ... and in this you will please what is capable of being loved in one another. This understanding alone nourishes your love, and in turn love will nourish your life together.

Teach and help each other to be independent. Wrongful dependency on one another breeds fear and cruelty. Instead, learn to depend on love, for love breeds love ... and real love is always independent and kind.

Don't try to change each other, either subtly or openly. This creates resentment. Instead, let the other find his or her way. This doesn't mean to condone whatever is seen as being wrong or obviously mistaken. It simply means don't condemn one another for a weakness, as love never lashes out but always strives to lift.

KEY LESSON

We cannot separate the problems of this world—including the pain endured in agreeing to honor, respect, and support those we love—from the awakening of a patience and kindness that can be born in us no other way.

Make the Great Exchange

The trees take in sunlight, transforming its vibrant energy into flowers that become fruits, giving rise to slow-spreading root systems that anchor both tree and soil, and growing leaves that shade the ground below for any creature seeking respite there from the midday heat.

Then there's the teenage squirrel—so filled to the brim with buoyant energy that it can't just walk but literally leaps from spot to spot like an over-wound children's top, bringing a smile to anyone who is there to share its joy. And, of course, there's the late spring rains that wash and refresh the drying grasses...that feed the mother doe nursing her newborn fawn.

On and on, this one great principle plays itself out before eyes that have yet to perceive its perfection...or no fear could rush in to cloud them: *real life is exchange*. It is a ceaseless cascade of timeless forces whose intelligent interactions sustain each level of creation, all in the service of an indivisible life whose unseen whole is greater than the sum of its parts.

This is the great model, the matrix of reality, as it is reflected from above to below. There are no exceptions to or exemptions from its rule or purpose. Any appearance to the contrary is just that, and whenever we break this rule—by clinging to who and what we have been in the face of any moment trying to show us that we've outlived the old model—we thwart its divine purpose, and then, much as weeds behind a broken plow, useless pain follows.

This understanding has direct implications for those who aspire to know the immortal Self. We are not meant to cling to the past—to seek there, for its sense of contentment or conflict, a feeling of ourselves. We can exchange this level of mind that struggles to know its place in life for the peace that comes in our atonement with life.

We are not meant to keep emotional accounts with others, to fill ourselves with disparaging thoughts of where they failed to meet our demands. Nor are we created to carry around with us the cruel and careless remarks of others, and this includes our regrets for where we may have done the same. We can exchange this nature of resentment, which lives to revisit disappointments, with a new and higher understanding that can no more feel punished by the sleeping actions of others than does a mountain feel pain in the midst of a thunderstorm.

We are not meant to keep our eye on some "tomorrow" from which we blindly borrow the false pleasure of what "might be." Such dreams serve nothing save the spiritually sleeping self: an imagined sense of "I" that always realizes, too late, that its hope in things seen is the same as tomorrow's sorrow. We can exchange its anxious struggle to complete itself in some "happier time" to come for the realization that our immortal Self is—and has always been—complete.

*In truth, who we really are is already complete,
yet this holiness can neither be known nor
kept any more than a raindrop can know that
its mother is some great distant sea or keep
itself from returning there, to its source.*

Watch the Waves of Thoughts
and Feelings Go By

Two very close friends, Karen and Sophie, went on a long-awaited vacation to a tropical island where, the first day, before that evening's grand welcoming luau, they spent the whole day playing in the ocean.

But early on that same evening, in the midst of all the great food and fantastic island music, Karen could barely keep her eyes open. Every part of her felt tired; in truth, she was feeling a bit of resentment towards her friend. For some reason, Sophie was showing no sign of slowing down, while all Sally wanted to do was to just collapse somewhere. It just didn't seem right!

So, collecting her thoughts—as well as her facial expression to not show any of the irritation she was feeling inside—Karen pulled Sophie aside and said, "I don't get it. You and I did the same thing all day: we lay on the beach and swam in the sea. Why aren't you as tired as I am? How come you seem to have energy to spare, and I'm dead in the water?"

"Well," said Sophie, "all I can think of is that while we were out playing around in the surf—which was for most the day—I enjoyed floating quietly between each of the waves and you—well, you didn't."

KEY LESSON

A tree has many leaves, and the wind touches all of them in way or another. Some shake, some quiver, and some hardly move at all. Yes, the tree knows their trembling, but neither the wind nor the leaves it stirs are the tree that feels their touch. Thoughts and feelings are like leaves: learning to watch them wave is much better than being carried away with every breeze.

Sow the Seeds of True
Self-Knowledge

Real life is not by the numbers; it is impossible to "know" and to grow at the same time. Yes, one can have a formula for a prescription drug or a recipe for a good green salad, but there is no system of thought that can stand up to the ever-shifting changes of real life, let alone meet those same changes fearlessly. The self that knows itself only through thought can never develop beyond the content of itself any more than a math equation can suddenly outgrow the pile of figures responsible for its form.

One of the reasons we want to know—in advance—how to do certain things, spiritually speaking, is that we want to save time in our spiritual search; we want to cut to the chase of how to end the conflict we have and arrive at the contentment we've imagined. We want to be at peace.

Among the many hidden contradictions in approaching the inner quest from such a mindset is the following: the more we try to save time—find a shortcut to higher consciousness—the more we actually create and slave beneath a false sense of time. We become further identified with the level of consciousness that creates the prison of time from which we hope to escape.

The truth is, *we can't know what to do in advance of any given moment.* Trying to meet life with predetermined ideas about to handle what unfolds before us—*before it does*—is like a downhill skier wanting to know where he will make his turns before he reaches the mountain he intends to ski! Add to this idea the fact that whenever ideals or systems of ideas go before us as measuring sticks, they are soon turned into a judge's bench from which we dispense some form of punishment on others (or upon ourselves) for not doing as we think ought to have been done.

Knowledge, regardless of how sophisticated, is a tool. It arises from and belongs to what has passed; it is the past put into a formula. As such, it embodies, defines, and relates us to life through what we, or others, have already come to know is true about reality.

But real life is not limited to what was; it is always new. *It is always now*. And while it may bring to light, under law, certain conditions or events that precede its appearance—what we call *karma*—it is more than just these forms alone, just as a flower in bloom is more than its newly opened petals.

Real life is the expression of living, intelligent forces that actively shape whatever they touch, as well as whatever reaches out to touch them. It might be said that each moment appears as it does—in whatever form or color, hard or soft, dark or light—to teach us about ourselves. How can we hope to learn what we must from such moments if we meet them already knowing how they should unfold? *No form is free*.

And just as we wouldn't mistake a ladder for being the same as the rooftop upon which we hope to view the stars, neither should we confuse knowledge for those innermost revelations that can come to us only through self-understanding. This level of genuine self-knowledge is never static. It places no demands on life; therefore, it fears nothing that life may reveal. It has nothing whatsoever to do with thoughts, plans, or otherwise imagined purposes.

Real self-knowledge is the unshakable ground of enduring peace and security. It is one with the present moment and a timeless intelligence that is at once aware of all that is unfolding within it, including what flowers as a result. This is your immortal Self.

KEY LESSON

Life is change; it is creation revealing itself. We can either realize our existence within its movement as a designated part of its divine design or we can continue to struggle with unwanted moments in the false belief that our pain over their temporary appearance proves we know how the story of our life is supposed to unfold.

Reaching Heaven's Shore

J ust as a ship lost at sea must make a course correction if it hopes to reach a safe harbor, so must
the aspirant be willing to be corrected by life for
there to be any hope of sighting heaven's shore. And
it isn't really so much that life itself corrects us as it is
that *it serves to reveal us to ourselves.* When it does, the
choice is ours whether to be self-correcting or deflect
the light of revelation that calls for us to change. And
when we consider that there can be no real correction
without this light shining within us, then—in some
strange and mysterious way—its action must be part
of our perfection process.

This is why refusing correction—the rejection of any moment that shows us the need to let go of who and what we've been up until that moment—is the same as refusing the invitation to realize a conscious relationship with one's immortal Self. After all, what else is the illumination of any dark, limiting state within us if not an invitation—by the same light that reveals it—to outgrow the parts of us that have agreed to give it a home?

Each time we let go and grow in this way, it isn't so much that we have learned something new as it is we've agreed to be made whole. With each correction that we can see needs to be made—and that we then agree to make within us—our heart and mind are brought into a new relationship with the light that reveals this need. In this way we not only join ourselves to the light, but it unites us. We are made holy.

Welcome correction; choose to be teachable. If the light can't touch you, it can't show you the wholeness of your immortal Self.

*We are never closer to realizing the next level
of our own higher possibilities than when,
by the light of a new awareness, we see some
old darkness within us and then agree that
we can no longer be what we have been.*

The Secret Source of Tomorrow's Sorrow

Dean and Charlie grew up together, attending the same local high school and college. Charlie married and divorced, then became a traveling salesman for a global cosmetics company.

Dean, on the other hand, never married and remained in his hometown taking on various jobs, none of which he would stay with for too long.

Even though the two men rarely spent time together over the ensuing years, their friendship remained intact.

After a particularly long sales trip overseas, Charlie was glad to be back on native soil and driving along quiet country roads. It always seemed to him that the open spaces were all the sweeter following so much time spent in crowded cities. He couldn't wait to get home and see his family. But halfway there he realized that would have to wait. He needed to pick up some batteries from the hardware store, so he decided to make a quick stop in town.

As he drove down Main Street, a hand-painted sign over a new shop caught his eye. It said *Dean's Custom Cabinets*.

No way! Charlie thought to himself. But pulling up in front of the large store window, his disbelief was confirmed. There, standing behind the counter, was his old friend Dean.

Charlie got out of the car, walked into the store, and said, "Hey, Dean! What in the heck is going on?"

"Hey, good buddy! When did you get back home?"

"Less than forty minutes ago," said Charlie, as he surveyed all the empty floor space. "Since when did you start making your own custom cabinets?"

Dean looked at him and said, "Well, I'm not sure you know this, but I did try my hand at making hand-crafted chairs—for a while, anyway."

"No, guess I never did hear about that," said Charlie. "Kinda hard to keep up with all the different things you try."

Dean lowered his voice and continued. "Yeah, that business didn't quite work out for me the way I hoped it would."

"Gee, Dean, sorry to hear it; I mean, what with you being a local boy and all that, seems folks 'round these parts would support most anything you'd put your hand to."

"Yeah, true enough, except for one little detail..."

Charlie raised his eyebrows in a question. "What's that?"

Dean chuckled to himself like he'd just heard a good joke. "Who would have thought it? Turns out I don't have a single woodworking skill in my whole body!"

At first Charlie couldn't believe his own ears. "Dean, I am so confused! With all due respect, what are you thinking, man? To handcraft custom cabinets takes even more woodworking skill than you need to make chairs!"

And then, looking directly at Charlie—as if it made perfect sense—Dean smiled his best good old country boy smile and said, "Sure enough, but this time I'm hoping things will work out better."

KEY LESSON

Hoping and waiting on some imagined time to come when you'll finally make that "positive change" in your life is like spending all your time complaining about the unkempt condition of your neighbor's garden while your own is overrun with weeds!

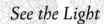

See the Light

W hy do you say that your color is white, when I can see that you are blue?" asked one who saw herself as being green but who was, in truth, a yellowish hue.

Then snapped back someone who had thought himself red but who was, in fact, nearly black, "*None of you are the color that you claim to be, and that's a fact!*"

So red, blue, black, and yellowish hue accused each other through the day and into the night. And, in the end, not one of them knew they had all missed seeing the light.

KEY LESSON

The rush to judge what we see as some character flaw in another human being is the speed at which the false self races to hide from itself a similar imperfection.

A Personal God:
Imagined or Real?

The notion of a "personal" God is due partly to the need of the divided mind to be consoled by *what it imagines* is required to complete it—which, by the way, can never be accomplished. Call it what you will, science or spiritual fact, the truth remains the same: *no opposite can complete itself.* And so the horror of religious wars became the substitute for the imagined salvation of a heaven that never came. It seems it's more palatable to hate one's neighbor than it is to confess that the love of one's imagined god is powerless to deliver one from fear and the hatred it breeds.

That said, those who have had an authentic spiritual awakening, who have realized their immortal Self, often describe a deep sense of a personal relationship with the Divine.

This is due to the actual nature of the revelations brought on by such an awakening: one can see by a supernal light that there is no separate self—no "me" apart from "thee." One is absorbed into a broader sphere of reality, along with its accompanying consolations and gifts.

In the end, metaphorically speaking, the aspirant reaches a point where not only is "belief" in a personal God unnecessary, but it is recognized as an obstruction to one's ongoing communion with one's immortal Self—a very real, timeless higher consciousness that includes divine love and compassion for all.

KEY LESSON

The great universal misperception that secretly drives human conflict, with all of its sorrow and pain, is that the meaning of life is to be found somewhere outside of one's own heart and mind.

How to Attract
Divine Attention

Over many years of living on a small mountaintop in southern Oregon, I have learned many invaluable spiritual lessons by observing the wildlife that share the forest in which my house sits sequestered. In truth, nature and her creatures are always exhibiting some of the most profound principles one can hope to learn. *The celestial hides itself in the common.* This realization of its tireless wisdom and grace never fails to reveal itself to those who learn to watch its goodness on display. A short personal story tells the tale of one such revelation.

Several years back I began throwing peanuts to some of the yakking Steller's jays that would regularly visit my birdfeeders. Over time I began learning some of the calls these birds make and gradually became able to call them to me from the woods around my house where they nest. Eventually I became friends with one of these jays that I came to name Heckle. Little did I know how prophetic his name would be!

As our relationship developed, Heckle eventually learned the following: if he would just land on one of the short benches sitting directly in front of my office window, and once perched there just stare at me longingly, eventually I'd have to get up from my chair and throw him some peanuts! He even learned to rustle and fluff up his feathers, as baby birds do to elicit the feeding response from their parents. I was powerless to resist him.

Now, almost every day—several times a day, in fact—Heckle shows up asking for a few treats. His persistence is impossible to describe. But this much I can tell you for a fact: when he sits there in front of me long enough, waiting on me as if it's a done deal, I'm a goner. His persistent nonverbal request always wins the action it's designed to elicit. And if our relationship reflects, in any way, the truth of what happens when a request is made consistently and persistently by one creature of another—which I am sure it is—*then how much more true would this same principle hold for someone who persistently and consistently asks to make contact with the Divine?*

Just as I am unable to refuse what this beautiful blue bird with his black crown asks of me, so is the very Goodness that reveals this relationship incapable of refusing a measure of its celestial crown to any and all who will persist in asking for it.

KEY LESSON

Attending to and completing what the present moment asks of you is the business of real life. In the silence of this relationship, the wisdom and wealth of your immortal Self is revealed and received all at once. A few of these timeless riches include a faith no fear can shake, an innocence no temptation can break, and a freedom that no unwanted moment in life can ever take from you.

Death Is Not the End of Life

We live in a stream of a living light that never stops pouring down upon us, even as it ceaselessly wells up from within us. The first part of this opening comment is obvious: sunlight streams down moment to moment upon our earth, vitalizing and nourishing all that it touches. And while this order of light allows us to see all the marvelous forms and colors that our physical eyes behold, there is another kind of light that is of a higher order.

In much the same way as sunlight reveals the world around us, this interior light illuminates the worlds within us and more. It is through the revelations that it alone makes possible—as it discloses whatever may be concealed within us—that we find and are nourished by an ever-expansive understanding of who and what we really are. We begin to realize our possibilities in life are as endless as this light that reveals them. Slowly it dawns upon us that standing in this light is the same as realizing the promise of an always new and self-liberating revelation.

For example, when we look out a window, our physical eyes may behold a field of green with a solitary tree that winter claimed three seasons past, now lying prone on the ground. Many small creatures have already moved into its hollows, claiming this place as their own. With a little grace, we may be touched by the beauty of this place and be bathed in the light of its meaning. But something far more beautiful than this simple pastoral scene is playing itself out before our eyes; there a deeper, higher meaning hidden in this moment, trying to teach us something about the truth of ourselves, about our immortal Self, if we will be present to its revelation.

That tree, even as it decays, bleeding its former strength and substance into the ground, isn't the end of the tree. *It's the end of the form that tree once took.* Everything that once constituted its character now becomes part of the grass; everything that's part of the grass, in turn, becomes part of the soil, and this enriched soil becomes a part of the next tree. The meaning of this revelation is one with its fear-ending fact: *death is not the end of life.*

Yet, for us, it seems as if our life comes to an untimely end over and over again. We all know that dreaded feeling of *oh no…my life is over!* Truth be told, this kind of experience is so old and worn out that *it* is what should have died long ago!

We've all died a thousand deaths and yet we're still here, hoping for life but fearing what we believe to be its partner: the appearance of some unwanted moment attended to by an inevitable sense of loss. This is the great illusion.

Real life serves the living without end. And, without end, it must constantly change itself to do this. But what do we serve when our heart and mind are as barren as a winter's tree, and all we know to do in those moments is turn on ourselves with a vengeance for not being what we imagine we should be?

For that matter, what do we serve when any relationship that defines us seems to betray us, leaving us alone with a suffering that, to be endured, must be blamed on another?

In these moments we serve a lower level of self that believes its very existence depends upon something outside of itself... so that we are indentured to a level of self *that believes it ends* when whatever it has identified with changes, *as must all things.*

No change in life marks the end of the immortal Self that, once again transformed, assumes a new form.

KEY LESSON

It's an eternal law: everything is always becoming something else. Real life is ceaseless transformation expressed through infinite forms. But within us lives the sleeping seed of a celestial self that alone can see—in spite of all evidence to the contrary—that nothing really changes.

The Show Goes On

It simply cannot be stated often enough: you have every reason to be encouraged about life. Just look around you. The Divine shows itself everywhere, and in all things we see by example that there is no death. Where do you see the end of anything beyond the mere passing of some individual form? The seemingly lifeless branch, barren in the hand of a winter's day past, becomes the budding star of each new spring season.

Life is the stage ... and death only a necessary character upon it whose presence adds the required tension and suspense for the viewing audience.

And yes, of course, as it must be with any play in due time, its curtains draw closed, the act at an end. But just as a closing curtain doesn't mean the end of the theater, so too can it be seen that the passing of life doesn't signal its disappearance.

The show goes on!

KEY LESSON

By love we overcome death, for death is an act of love, not the end of it.

Doing Your Part in
the Divine Plan

Great uncertainty surrounds the whole idea of self-realization. When it comes to the possibility of being in conscious relationship with what is divine—of discovering your immortal Self—what everyone wants to know is "how?" From that point it seems the confusion boils down to this question: *Is there or is there not a plan of some kind? Are there organized lessons of some order that one can follow all the way to everlasting freedom?*

The answer is no and yes. And, in the end, the only person who succeeds in realizing the truth of Self is the one who will struggle to understand what only seems to be an irreconcilable contradiction.

St. Theophan the Recluse said that divine grace will not act within us if we don't make efforts to obtain it, but to this idea he *also added* that human efforts alone are incapable of producing anything spiritually stable or permanent within us. Therefore, he goes on to say, that the divine result, the fulfillment of our realization, is "to be obtained by a combination of effort and grace." Here's what this means to those seeking the Kingdom of the Divine:

Effort—any kind of "plan"—without grace is useless. Grace—unattended by effort and its inherent humiliation—produces illusion. Just as there must be a marriage between the aspiring soul and the timeless Spirit that gives it life, so must there be a union between spiritual sweat, sacrifice, and the fruit of what that interior work reveals.

To understand this requirement of self-realization is to recognize the absolute necessity of an authentic teacher and wisdom school. Without the new insights and access to the higher self-knowledge thus provided, the willing aspirant has no viable tools with which to work, nor does he or she receive the vital reminders—and encouragements—that are needed in order to renew the specialized work required to become self-realized.

Without the spirit that governs the dissemination and directed application of these specialized tools, they prove useless, not unlike giving a book on calculus to a child who still plays with a ruler, imagining it as a seesaw. *No one finds the true upper way without true guidance.* And yet, on the other hand, seemingly in direct opposition to all stated above, we have this beautiful fact of life:

Within the lowly acorn resides the "plan" for the great oak tree it is destined to become; in a manner of speaking, one could say that the oak tree is the acorn realized, assuming it's given the conditions it needs to succeed in fulfilling its plan. Which leads us to this highly encouraging fact as concerns life in all kingdoms, above and below: in every seed resides a living plan placed within it at the same moment of its creation.

This means that hidden in the center of you is the seed of self-realization—the possibility of discovering that who you really are is part of a divine plan.

If you can remember the first time you fell in love, it's pretty much guaranteed that you didn't run around asking others, "What's the plan?" Love itself was your guide, and the actions she prescribed moment to moment flowed into and through you; they were provided by a love that wanted nothing more from you than your willingness to be its instrument. The rest was literally done for you, and there was never a question of how this love would turn out. No future fears clouded your original contentment; it was enough just to love and to be loved. That doesn't mean there weren't difficulties, but they were recognized as being a necessary part in the play of love perfecting itself.

Think of some great artist, any master you admire past or present, then consider, carefully, what it took for that individual to realize and then embody such an immense gift. Let me summarize the process of such perfection: love, sweat, sacrifice, revelation, and its enactment.

So, is there a plan for self-realization?

The answer is … yes *and* no. And it all depends on you.

KEY LESSON

Whenever we place any form of mental or physical consolation—be this food, friends, religious icons, some foolish purchase—ahead of our need to realize the indwelling Divine, we may be assured of the following result: the only thing that will change for us in the days ahead is what we cling to to help get us through the night.

The Patience to Possess Your Soul

All that is moves through and expresses itself in cycles. Think of the seasons: each spring there is a stirring, the promise of a birth yet to come; we see, revealed before us, the appearance of possibilities that were formerly at rest. The summer brings the fulfillment of spring's promise in its plenitude. Come the fall, natural forces subside; there is a reversal in the direction of energies. Enter the winter, and all movement halts; everything rests in solitude entombed in its last form prior to this cycle. And then everything starts again.

Whenever we are graced with a glimpse of truth and see its veracity and feel the first warmth of its possibility stirring in us, a seed of celestial possibility is awakened in our soul in that same moment. And though its fruition is yet to come, something in the ground of our soul senses its abundance; there is a silent but strengthening yearning, much as one might imagine a seed's first effort to reach up and touch the light of the sun whose radiance has awakened it.

Slowly, steadily—as is true of any seed still in the early days of being in the dark earth—we are moved by what we know not, save for a sweet intuition of its beauty and strength. If we remain quietly receptive, we gradually realize what each of these seed moments alone makes possible: the flowering of new self-understanding, with all its abundance and peace. And then, as it must, the forces responsible for the fulfillment of things yield to a time for rest and reconciliation; solitude descends, and we take rest in a form that will be the next seed.

All are subject to the laws that govern and maintain these greater cycles of life. Active gives way to passive, passive heralds a return to activity; all must be reconciled and then start again.

Learning to observe, recognize, and honor these cycles as aspects of our own consciousness liberates us from being unconsciously identified with whatever may momentarily appear and disappear within them. Our fear of change is replaced with a wonder of what new good they have come to herald. In this way, we gain the patience needed to possess and perfect our soul. We find a new order of freedom for having realized that while everything in life must come and go, the source of light by which we now witness this parade of cycles has no end.

KEY LESSON

The mind emptied of its attachments fears nothing, while the mind full of itself spends its time fearfully watching over everything.

Free Yourself from the Unseen Influence of Dark Forces

The dark powers that presently govern this world are secretly dedicated to the denigration of character, which they slowly achieve through attrition, glorification of social imitation, and a growing sense of discouragement felt by anyone who sees the promise of humanity slipping away in creeping mediocrity.

Whenever any government anywhere promotes and celebrates the idea of reduced individual responsibility to the point where it becomes a cultural ideal—so that its people are actually thankful to the powers that be for diminishing their own higher possibilities—so dawns a new dark age, which is, as it turns out, the goal of the same dark powers that helped to usher it in.

We are wrongly led to believe that life makes us into the kind of person we are. In truth, it's our level of self-understanding that makes life what it is for us! This is why nothing can really change for us until we see that trying to change some condition in life without first changing the consciousness responsible for its appearance is like blaming the mirror for what we don't like seeing in it!

*The Easy Way Is
the Wrong Way*

Early one morning, just as the sun is rising and
throwing its gentle light through the bars of
the one window that graces his prison cell,
Armand is awakened by a sound he has never heard
before. He knows immediately that it isn't coming
from the ocean that lies somewhere outside the prison walls; the sound of its waves and the wind that
carries them to his ears have become his only friends,
even though he can see neither of them due to the
height of his cell window. His mind races; a faint
smile comes over his face as he thinks *I must be losing
my mind.* But there it is again, only louder; there can

be no doubt about it: a distinct scratching noise is coming up from out of the hard dirt floor of his cell.

A heartbeat later, the ground farthest away from the cell window starts moving, and, in another instant, it breaks wide open and from out of it pops, like a gladiola, a head with long hair and a beard.

Before Armand can say a word, the man silences him and says, "Hush! Don't be afraid. My name is Edmond. I have much to explain, and we haven't much time! I'm one of several political prisoners living here who has been digging an escape tunnel for over two years now. Just beyond the walls of your cell sits the ocean—and our way out of this hellhole."

He pauses long enough to make sure that Armand is getting the big picture.

"We've tunneled as far as we can without being caught, so now it's on your shoulders. Are you following me?"

Armand shakes his head as if to say no, but Edmond continues on anyway.

"Listen to me carefully—that is, if you want to get out of this place alive. Here's what remains to be done."

Shaking the dirt from his hair, Edmond rises slightly out of the hole he's standing in, raises his arm, and points his finger towards the wall in Armand's cell that has the window in it.

"Dig six feet down from right there, head due east, and less than two hundred yards from that spot is freedom for all of us!"

Armand says, "Yes...yes, I will do it! Anything to see my friends and family again."

To which Edmond responds, "Great! I'll check back with you by the new moon—sooner if it's safe to do so."

Sometime later, again just before sunrise, Edmond pops his head back up through the floor in Armand's cell and, using only his eyes, asks how things are going. Armand smiles broadly and says, proudly, "I've done it!"

Edmond quietly exclaims, "Good heavens, that was fast!" And, without wasting a moment, he climbs out of his hole, races across the cell, and dives into the opening of the new tunnel he had asked Armand to dig. Less than five minutes later, Edmond pops back up out of the hole with a look of sheer horror on his face.

"By all that's holy, man, what have you done?"

Armand looks at Edmond, wondering what his problem is, somewhat shocked at his negative reaction. "What do you mean? What's wrong?"

"Do you remember what we discussed—what I told you to do? *Do you?*"

Not waiting for Armand to answer, Edmond continues. "I told you to dig in the direction towards the ocean. The tunnel you've dug leads directly back into the center of the prison yard!"

Armand just looks at him for a moment and says, as if it makes all the sense in the world, "Yes, I know, but *the digging was easier in that direction.*"

KEY LESSON

Here's the real reason why it's so important to always go the extra mile—to do what you don't want to do or feel like you can't do— whenever it comes to your work to be free: there is no other way for you to make contact with, and then call upon, an indwelling limitless resource that will only reveal itself to you after you've exhausted your own.

Step Into the Unknown

In the life of all who aspire to realize a conscious relationship with the Divine, there comes a time when their journey reaches what seems to be a complete impasse.

These encounters of the unwanted kind represent distinct stages along the inner path. In truth, they are points of initiation resulting from certain revelations that lead directly to these moments. However, their inevitable outcome is always the same: the seeker loses faith in "things seen." He is no longer able to believe in either a heaven to come—as attained by his own efforts—nor can he believe any longer in his own "powers" that have proven, time and time again, to be powerless. In the parting of these mists appears what looks like a spiritual dead end, and so dawns a dark night of the soul replete with its utter sense of emptiness.

These unwanted moments are actually a doorway to the Divine; each marks a secret entrance into the immortal Self—a threshold that few reach and fewer still dare cross over. After all, when one reaches the point where the chosen path proves pointless, where else is there to go? There is no road going forward; the known way is expired because nothing waits ahead but emptiness. Clearer still, nothing of value remains behind. There is no going back. One's heart is dry; the mind is barren save for the negative thoughts popping out of it, deftly pointing the finger of blame!

The true aspirant has no choice but to wait in what seems to be a spiritual wasteland. He is doubly stricken and without consolation, for his is both the poverty and the paradox of knowing there's nothing he can do to change his situation. Nevertheless, he also knows that this new self-understanding is the fruit of *all the revelations leading up to it*! Somehow, he is right where he's supposed to be—that is, *if* his wish is to learn the lessons that await him there.

As he consents to be blind, his inner eyes open. Now he sees that regardless of how dark or empty any given moment may first appear, it acts only as a herald of the living light he needs to see his way home to the Divine.

And so, summoning a will not his own, he steps into the unknown.

KEY LESSON

By whatever name you may give it, there is only one journey to the immortal Self: it is the walk into and all the way through oneself.

Reclaim These Two Spiritual Treasures

In this life we are only given two things that are purely our own to use: attention and time.

Attention

When we give our attention to something, it helps us realize—through that relationship—some quality or character within ourselves of which we were unaware only the moment before.

For instance, give your attention to just how deep runs the star-studded night sky above you, and you're instantly brought into an awareness of a corresponding timelessness within you. The depths of an endless night sky serve to reveal you to you; this is its spiritual purpose.

Here we glimpse the interior meaning of the much-beloved idea that beauty is in the eye of the beholder. The eye and what it beholds mirror one another, validating yet another ancient axiom: the observer is the observed. This understanding explains, in part, why Eastern traditions stress the idea of polishing the heart's mirror. The purer the heart, the more perfect its reflection of love.

Time

In this world of passing time, we are carried along in a river of ceaselessly changing relationships created by ever-converging forces beyond our control. Yet each and every one of these relationships holds the promise, the possibility, of a new revelation; and, as we've seen, each revelation reflects some aspect of one's immortal Self.

It is through standing in the flow of time—by watching how its waters wash away all that they touch, including our days on earth—that a true need to know what is timeless appears within us.

This new and interior longing, along with the revelations that have helped give birth to its awakening, changes what we value. Our time on earth takes on new meaning and purpose, for now we seek a whole new level of self that can never be taken or stolen from us.

Sadly, most of us squander our gifts of time and attention. Rather than learning to be in command of our attention, which is the same as using our time for its highest purpose—the realization of our immortal Self—we hand it over to almost anything that floats by in the river of time.

Either we struggle to "make" things happen or we wait hoping change will come; regardless of our approach to life, it never fails to give us something to think about or some event to stimulate us. Then we call that momentary relationship—and the passing sense of self it produces in us—"life." Yes, of course: this *is* one order of life, and we all have it…until we realize, often too late, that it has had us all along.

We have no choice about being born into this world of passing time, but we do have a choice whether or not we remain a captive of its inherent fears and sorrow.

Invite the light of your longing for what is everlasting to show you the futility of serving passing time. You are here on earth to realize an entirely different purpose to your life—a beautiful, noble, sacrificial purpose. But there's only way to have this higher calling revealed to you: you must give your attention to it moment by precious moment.

Stay awake. Stay in your body. Don't let your mind drag you around, always talking to you, telling you the meaning of what you see. Learn to master your attention. It will, in turn, teach you the real purpose and proper use of your time here on earth. Master time and attention, and you stand at the doorway to the Divine. Step through it and behold your immortal Self.

KEY LESSON

We will make detailed preparations for a single day off, lay out careful plans for an evening meal, and spend untold moments worrying over what we should wear, but few of us rarely take the time we need preparing our interior life to receive the impressions that give our soul its substance and meaning.

*Lead Us from the
Unreal to the Real*

Bill and Mike are pretty good neighbors. Their friendship is based on occasional family barbecues and the yearly championship football games when Mike comes over to watch the game at Bill's house on his large screen TV.

One morning, looking out his living room window, Mike notices that Bill and his wife and kids are out early setting up tables in their driveway. Bill is pulling boxes from the garage while the rest of his family unloads them, stacking the tables high with everything under the sun.

"Must be a yard sale," Mike thinks to himself, and before he knows it, he's walked over to their driveway and is busy examining everything on display. Then his eye catches sight of something that he really wants, but he can't understand why Bill would be selling it. After all, he had once asked if he could borrow it, and Bill had said, "Oh sure, just leave your driver's license and a $50 deposit!" Only Mike could tell that Bill wasn't really kidding.

Still, there it is, right in front of him: an absolutely beautiful color-plated coffee table book, *The Amazing Wild American Bluebird*. Both he and Bill are amateur birders, and this highly sought-after limited edition was something anyone who loved bluebirds would be proud to own. The thought comes to him that maybe Bill put this out by mistake and that maybe he should point it out to him. But, then again, why look a gift-horse in the mouth? A moment later, book in hand, he walks over to greet Bill.

"Hey, man, what's going on?"

"Mike, nice to see you; not too much … just getting rid of some stuff I don't really need anymore. How's life for you? Wife and kids okay?"

"Sure, you know the drill. Mind if I ask you a quick question?"

"What's up?"

From behind his back, where he has been more or less hiding it, Mike pulls out the oversize bluebird book, showing it to Bill. "I thought you loved this book—like it was one of your favorite things in the world?"

Mike waits to see Bill's expression, figuring that a strong reaction to the book being in his hands would mean that it got put out for sale by accident. But nothing...Bill's still smiling.

So Mike continues. "I mean, last time I was over—a couple of months ago, if I'm not mistaken—I asked if I could borrow it and you said something like, 'Sure, but you'll have to leave a deposit!'"

Bill laughs out loud, somewhat embarrassed. "Yeah, sorry about that, Mike. It is true, though; that book always was near and dear to me."

"Well, what happened, if you don't mind saying so?"

Taking a deep, measured breath, as if thinking through what he wants to say next, Bill says, "Well, the kids and I finally got around to building a beautiful little house for the bluebirds—you know, the kind you can actually see into without bothering the birds. And now"—a big, warm grin fills his face—"well, now I'm proud to say I have a family of bluebirds nesting right outside my living room window!"

"Gee, that's great, Bill… I'm happy for you, for sure. You must be just thrilled. But what's that got to do with you selling your favorite book about bluebirds?"

"Don't you see, Mike? It's no longer of any use to me."

Mike looks closely into Bill's eyes, trying to figure out what he's saying between the lines. "No, Bill… to be honest, I don't get it. Help me out here."

"Think about it, man… I don't need a book of pictures anymore. *I have the real thing now.*"

Real life never stops starting over, but before one can dwell in this this newness—and know its unencumbered freedom—one must let go of any and all attachments in the past that produce a painful sense of self.

The Unexpected Blessing
in Being Reviled

The only thanks you can expect from others who see you choosing to serve something higher than your own self-centered interests—which includes no longer enabling or indenturing yourself in the service of their inflated self-images—is their accusation that you have wronged them. And, as a rule, following these assertions—like dust does the wind that stirs it into the air—comes the demand that you justify your actions or else be found guilty of having turned against them.

If you want to see the real nature behind these thinly veiled threats, just quietly refuse to explain yourself when others hint that you're somehow being dishonorable. Although it won't seem so at first, your reward will be to watch their smiling faces turn upside down, and—no longer able to maintain its socially contrived disguise—to see therein a dark, fearful, miserable little "self" that can't help but despise anything or anyone who dares reveal it to itself.

The blessing in these moments of being reviled—when you see revealed the desperation and destitution of your accuser—is the spiritual liberation that comes only with the clarity of seeing who you can no longer be and what you can no longer serve.

KEY LESSON

When all is said and done, what matters
isn't whether the world—or anyone in it—
loves us or approves of us; what matters is
what we love, for that is what determines
the true and final course of our lives.

Honesty Is the Best Policy

If there is one essential characteristic or element most needed to ensure the success of those who seek the immortal Self, it is self-honesty. Without true integrity—from the inside out—it is impossible for the aspirant to come into a conscious, living relationship with the Divinity within.

This is why when it comes to life, our relationships with others, and our relationship with ourselves, honesty is always the best policy. Unfortunately, it seems that more and more these days, honesty is out of vogue. In times of unchecked and socially glorified acts of selfishness, honesty is seen more as an impediment to one's happiness than it is honored as the path to being a truly successful human being.

But what exactly is "honesty"? What does it mean, and what has it to do with honoring one's deepest and highest aspirations in this life of ours?

In *Webster's American Dictionary of the English Language* (circa 1828), we learn that honesty is "a moral rectitude of heart" or "upright conduct."

Rectitude is defined as "literally straightness, but not to material things; exact conformity to truth, to the rules prescribed either by divine or human law."

Of note here is that in every scripture worldwide you will find some statement along the same lines of this sentiment taken from Matthew in the New Testament: "Strait is the gate, and narrow is the way, which leadeth unto life, and few there be that find it."

And then there's that old expression from days gone by where someone is asking to be told the truth of his situation: "Give it to me straight, doc!" In other words, "Tell me the reality of my situation; I need you to be *real* with me."

The following may seem obvious, but apparently it's not: the flattering images we have and hold about ourselves are not honest. Yes, they seem real enough to the dreamer within us. But this sleeping self exists only in the world of imagination; as such, it can never be transformed or transfigured in any meaningful way. Nothing real touches it, and it touches nothing other than the unceasing stream of thoughts that provide its false sense of life. Let's look at an example to better understand this last idea.

Imagine a small stream-fed pond suddenly cut off from the body of life-giving waters that created it. For a while it teems with life, but its destiny—along with everything that has carved out a life within it—is to dry out and pass from existence. Were the little pond to remain connected to the flow of the stream, it would be continually refreshed and recharged by the rise and fall of those waters; changes within it would occur naturally, effortlessly, because it would be acted on by a source of life greater than itself.

In much the same way, we are intended to be made new; ours is the capacity for a conscious relationship with the celestial energies whose flow creates, reveals, replenishes, and sustains all that it touches. Think of self-honesty as one of the main ways we can align ourselves with these everlasting "waters." Seeing ourselves as we are recharges our divine wish to be one with what is incorruptible—a wish that is strengthened each time we catch ourselves deliberately painting a picture of ourselves that we know is false, self-serving, or just plain misleading.

On the other hand, every time we refuse or otherwise deny the truth of ourselves—anytime we cover up what we see living within us—we effectively cut ourselves off from this ever-flowing stream of real life. It is our singular task and true purpose in life to stand in the light of these divine energies and welcome all that they reveal. They alone have the power to transfigure and set free the consciousness into which they pour.

Almost all of us know these timeless words: "Then you will know the truth, and the truth will set you free." Perhaps now we understand them a little better; let us learn to welcome that little light within us that would show us the straight and true way back home to our immortal Self.

Honesty heals; lies hurt. In these four words live all one needs to know and practice—that is, assuming one wishes to be whole, harmless, loving, and true.

See Through This
Dark Attraction

A father and his two young children were on their way to visit some relatives upstate when they happened to drive by a small carnival set up just off the interstate highway. The kids immediately started begging their dad to pull over, get some snacks, and maybe go on a few rides, just to break the monotony of the long road trip. He was pretty tired himself after four straight hours of driving, so he said, "Sure, sounds like fun!" A few cheers went through the car, and ten minutes later they were standing at the entrance to the "Big Show."

The first thing that caught the father's eye was that one of the attractions had almost half of the entire Saturday crowd standing in line to get into it. The rest of the rides were, at best, sparsely attended.

As they walked around, enjoying a few snacks and jumping on a couple of rides together, the father couldn't stop wondering why that one attraction—what looked like a common house of mirrors—was more popular than anything else there; in his mind, there was no accounting for it. But, seeing as how the line was just as long as it was when they arrived, he decided to leave the question unanswered.

After a last caramel apple, washed down with some "homemade" lemonade, everyone headed back to the car to finish the rest of the drive north. But, just as they were leaving, the father noticed an unusually tall, dark man barking orders to a few of the carnie roughnecks standing around near the exit gate. He felt certain that this must be the owner and, a moment later, kids in tow, he walked over and said hello. After a cursory introduction, he got down to asking what had been on his mind since they had arrived at the carnival.

"I was wondering if you'd mind answering a small question I have about one of your attractions?"

The man just nodded as if to say okay, so he continued.

"That one ride over there"—he pointed to the house of mirrors—"is at least three times more popular than any other on the grounds. In fact, I can still see people arriving to get in. What's that all about ... I mean, with no disrespect, a house of mirrors is just, well, a house of mirrors, isn't it?"

The carnie owner smiled back at him. "Nope, not *that* one," he said with absolute confidence. "You see, before I retired and bought this carnival on wheels, I was a licensed electrician who also happened to be a bit of a backyard inventor. At any rate, one day while I was tinkering around, I figured out a way—using small pulses of electrostatic energy—to change the reflective surface of each of the mirrors in the house." He paused for just a second, giving the father a chance to absorb the novelty of this idea.

"Anyway," he went on, "these low-charge bursts of energy fire off randomly every three to seven seconds, and when they pulse, the mirror's surface that they're wired into instantly changes whatever is being reflected in it." He stopped again, apparently smiling at his own ingenuity.

"So," he continued, "what happens with each of these random micro-pulses is that the person standing in front of that mirror suddenly sees himself in a completely new way; he or she has a new shape, a different face, that's never the same twice in a row." And again he smiled to himself, as if he knew a joke he wasn't telling.

After a moment or two, allowing all that he's been told to sink in, the father says, "Well, I guess that does make *your* house of mirrors unlike any other, but"—and then, carefully collecting his thoughts so as to not appear rude or, worse, stupid—"to be perfectly honest, I still don't get it. What's so special about mirrors that keep changing the way you appear in them? Where's the big attraction in that?"

The answer that came tumbling out of the carnival owner's mouth was as stunning in its simplicity as the father knew, sadly, that it was also shockingly true:

"People never get tired of looking at themselves."

KEY LESSON

No reflection is real. If an image could satisfy the desire that created it, then a picture of food would ease the pain of hunger and painting a smile on one's face in the mirror would smooth away any bitterness in the heart.

Find Lasting Freedom in Spiritual Stillness

On this one point all saints, sages, and illumined beings agree: there is nothing as certain as silence, stillness, and solitude to introduce you to the divinity within.

The first step in learning to be still isn't really an action at all, meaning that it's nothing like we might ordinarily think of doing when we want our world to stop spinning like a top. Being still begins with being quietly aware that whatever seems to be whirling around you is really just a reflection of the world of unseen reactions within you. Here we come upon one of the cardinal rules of realizing higher consciousness.

If you will remember this timeless injunction, you'll never find yourself lost for an explanation as to why any moment in your life appears as it does to you—or what to do about it:

The inner determines the outer.

In these five short words lives all the power you need to transcend any unwanted experience in your life, starting with this realization: what we receive in—and from—each moment of life is inseparable from our perception of it.

To help make this last idea clear, imagine a man who complains to his friend that for the whole day he has felt dark and gray, only to be reminded that he's wearing his dark gray sunglasses. Once he realizes that his sense of self is being negatively affected because of his dark lenses, he removes them. Now he sees the light, in all meanings of the word. He understands that before he could alter his gloomy experience of that day, he had to first change what was causing him to see it that way. Any other action was not only doomed to fail but could only serve to lead him further and further away from the one realization that set him free. Which brings us to this next cardinal rule:

There is nothing to do, only something to see.

Blind reactions based on an incomplete understanding of your circumstances always sow the seeds of yet other unwanted moments yet to come. Everything you "do" in this manner only serves to create more of the very disturbance that you had set out to silence in yourself. This is always true because resistance to any disturbance in yourself ensures its repetition.

Trying to escape a noisy mind may seem as if you're putting some real distance between yourself and all its chattering, but here's why this kind of action never really resolves the problem. Only a noisy mind wants to get away from itself—something that it can never do any more than the tip of a pencil can escape the eraser on the other end that it fears is trying to rub it out!

Think for a moment: does silence fear any noise or does it just let it pass through unmolested? This means any frantic wish to be still must belong to a part of your lower nature that's already disturbed— one that is trying to hide its pain by sending you to look for peace! So now you know the truth.

There's nothing you need to do in the face of anything that frightens you other than agree to be still and see it. This order of awareness has its own power; all you need to do is place yourself where this living light can act for you, upon you. That's the first step; take it, and then see how the Divine takes the next step for you. Watch it to prove—over and over again— that there's nothing you can bring into its stillness greater than its ability to transform and transcend it all at once and once and for all.

KEY LESSON

Your true self is a creative silence, a ground of perfect stillness from which all disturbances appear and to which they return if left alone. The clearer this revelation becomes, the more confident you become that being still is the same as the power to solve any problem before it begins.

Pride Comes
Before the Fall

It was late one evening. Tim was walking home from a small dinner party to celebrate his second promotion in less than a year. As he crossed a dark alleyway, looking down it to be sure he was in no danger, he noticed a man who was sitting there on the ground with his back propped up against a brick wall.

It wasn't the first time Tim witnessed what he knew to be human misery, and he knew it wouldn't be the last. His heart went out to this poor fellow, even as he felt even more grateful for his own good fortune in life. But as he walked on, something in the back of his mind was bothering him, trying to get his attention. Within the space of another ten steps, he realized what was troubling him. At first he thought to himself *no, that can't possibly be ...* But as his mind focused itself on the image of the man in the alley, it became clear to him he had to go back. Though it seemed highly unlikely, everything in him felt like he knew this unfortunate man.

As he retraced his steps, his mind began to call up distinct images—personal snapshots from a year earlier that had been stashed in the back of his memory. Both he and the man he thought he recognized, Saul, worked for the same major corporation. They were in a constant state of competition, a battle really, over who would be promoted to a junior partnership in the company.

Tim could feel his body tensing with each recollection of the conflict that existed between them and how what had started as a close friendship had turned into a conflict-ridden relationship. He knew that, given the chance, Saul would throw him under the bus in the wink of an eye. But what bothered him most of all was that Saul didn't have a repentant bone in his body. Even when caught red-handed doing something underhanded to gain an advantage, he showed no remorse.

There seemed to be no end to his arrogance, right up to and including the moment when Tim was selected for the partnership. He could remember the hateful look on Saul's face and how, a moment later, Saul lashed out at everyone gathered there for the announcement—including the CEO, who fired him on the spot.

Tim realized he hadn't thought of Saul much at all over the last twelve months and certainly hoped that it wasn't really him sitting there in the alley.

As Tim got closer, he could see by the dim light of an overhead security lamp that it was, indeed, Saul. His clothes were filthy, his face was unshaven, and his eyes were sallow, almost the color of the dark brick upon which he was leaning.

"Oh my God, Saul, is that you?"

Saul raised his head to see Tim and just shook his head no.

"Let me help you up, man. Come on—I know we can get this straightened out."

A snarl came across Saul's face like something one would see on a cornered animal. He snapped, "Leave me alone; everything was fine until you got here!"

Ignoring his comment, Tim asked, "What's happened to you...how on earth did you end up here like this?"

Saul's face softened for just a moment, but it was quickly overtaken by a hardness that startled Tim, causing him to take a step back.

With sarcasm dripping from his lips, Saul asked, "You wanna know how I got here, *old pal*? Is that what you're asking me?"

Almost afraid to say yes, Tim managed to nod his head in the affirmative.

Saul braced his back up against the wall, staring in defiance at Tim. And then, in a voice filled with pride, he said, "I did it *my* way..."

The dark and painful pretense of human arrogance exists only as it does because of how distanced we've become from the immense, divine mystery of our own being. The more we awaken to the depth of this mystery, the more our character realizes its natural supernal humility.

Freedom from the Fear
of Feeling Powerless

Ｔrue spiritual "power" isn't the ability to imagine and implement an endless series of new solutions to old problems. Rather, it is a radical new and higher form of self-understanding, one that illuminates and transcends *our unconscious need to have any painful problems at all*. Which would you rather have: a personal fire truck and a fire to put out every day or a life free of painful flames?

The truth is, most of us spend a great deal of our time struggling in vain to sort out one conflict or another with others, with the world, or within ourselves. Part of our ever-developing plan to "win" these wars requires us to acquire new powers that we imagine will end our suffering once and for all. But past experience proves these exercises to be pointless: the *very thing* that we set out to obtain to make us fearless, to relieve our stress, soon becomes the source of a new fear and a new pressure!

Not unlike an addict taking his drug of choice to release himself from the cyclical pain of his addiction, we continue to seek powers outside ourselves to free us from feeling powerless in the face of what pains us. It's obvious that no drug the addict wants can free him from wanting drugs. What isn't so obvious, at least not yet, is the following: each power that we imagine will liberate us only strengthens our false belief that the power we need to be free is to be found somewhere outside of us.

We have no idea of the power with which we have been endowed. Within us dwells the possibility of realizing a level of consciousness whose freedom has no contingencies, one that cannot fall apart even when the conditions in our lives seem to come undone.

This special kind of power has nothing to do with being able to control or manipulate conditions outside of us. We're talking about a completely different kind of power: authority over our own negative reactions.

Consider the ability to possess ourselves as opposed to trying to possess things or relationships through which we have a measure of security. The power to possess ourselves can't be granted by anyone or anything outside of us. All powers of the worldly order are powerless to grant us what our heart of hearts wants more than anything else: *to be quietly in charge of our own heart and mind.*

The next time you're overcome with feeling as if you are powerless, take this one interior action and watch that fear disappear: instead of looking at what your fear is telling you is greater than your power to deal with it—i.e., a failing relationship, a brewing storm, or a pending loss of some kind—*look instead at the part of you that wants you to believe that who you are is inadequate to meet the challenge at hand.* Then remember the following truth:

All feelings of being powerless are the false projections of a frightened level of self that is not you.

Real spiritual power is knowing that no moment is greater than your divine right to call upon an indwelling light that transforms any darkness it touches into something bright, true, and good for all.

Nothing in the universe can make us relive some painful moment as long as we choose to live from the higher understanding that no old dark thought has the power to define us, let alone drag us down. Without our unconscious consent, the past is powerless to punish us in the present moment.

Stop Useless Suffering
Before It Begins

If there could be only one idea—a lamp whose light could show the aspirant of real life the way out of the prison of dark thoughts and punishing feelings—it would surely be this: *your true self doesn't win in life by overpowering problems but by revealing they never really existed as you once believed they did.*

Truths such as this can be difficult to accept. Tell some people the basis of their present mental or emotional pain is a negative byproduct of a mind trapped in an illusion and, as a rule, their response is to cling all the more tightly to their suffering. With few exceptions, the justification of their pain is as follows:

given what they have had to endure, there is no alternative but this, their pain. So before we go any further, let's set the record straight:

Many things that have happened and that continue to happen in our world are, at best, dark and difficult to deal with. Let there be no question about this: sleeping human beings do terrible things to others, as well as to themselves. Compassion and her older sister Empathy seem to be on an extended vacation so that suffering grows unchecked. But the key point here for those seeking the Self that never dies is that passing events in themselves do not have the power to make us suffer. It is our negative reactions that first blind us, bind us, and then hurl us into a world of hurt.

The proof of this crucial finding that events themselves are not the source of our psychological suffering is found in the inspiring life stories of many people throughout history. One by one, we learn how individuals facing impossibly painful conditions not only transcend the hardships they face but emerge from them in some way transfigured. And what one can do, all may do; the victory of a single soul over any darkness lights the path for all who follow. A few real-life stories help illustrate this beautiful truth.

Not so many years ago, a brilliant young athlete was injured in an accident that left him paralyzed. Instead of falling into despair, he went on to help other young people who were similarly injured to overcome their sense of loss and lead healthy, productive lives.

In an interview about how the accident had changed his life and how his loss had come to enrich the lives of others like himself, he made some very revealing comments. He told the reporter that without the accident that took his legs, his eyes never would have been opened to see there was a whole new dimension of life just waiting for him to be awakened to it. His life-shattering experience had so transformed all that he knew about life before it that, if given a choice, he wouldn't change anything that had happened.

How did he come out on top of life conditions that tend to bury most others? Rather than be dragged down by it, he agreed to learn the life-elevating lesson that lies hidden in all unwanted moments.

Choosing this right path in the face of his pain brought him immeasurable rewards. For instance, he came to realize, as we must, that his true Self is not tied to his physical body or to the outcome of any unwanted circumstances. His awakening to truths such as this fulfilled him in ways that no man-made trophy ever could. Although in the eyes of the world he had become more limited, in fact his universe had expanded to realize a new sense of freedom beyond anything he might have hoped for in his former state.

A devastating event that could have sown the seeds of bitter regret and resentment grew instead into a soul-ennobling opportunity that gave him a whole new way to look at his life. An old Arabic saying suggests the secret behind this triumph:

The nature of rain is the same, but it makes thorns grow in the marshes and flowers in the gardens.

In his inspiring book *Man's Search for Meaning*, Viktor Frankl describes his experiences as a prisoner in a Nazi death camp. While many became embittered and hardened in their captivity, some were able to transcend even their horrifying circumstances to develop a relationship with a higher power. No longer tied to the meanness and cruelty of the world in which they found themselves physically, they achieved a spiritual understanding that lifted their lives—and others around them in the same dark situation—far beyond the reach of man's inhumanity to man. Such transformation is largely incomprehensible to those who believe their anger at some injustice makes their hatred righteous. The spiritually blind suffer only themselves but always "see" others as being responsible for why they feel the pain and sorrow that they do.

To be able to see *any* life event—good or bad—as a vehicle to help transport us from our present level of understanding to a higher one requires that we develop a new relationship with these unwanted events in our lives. *Instead of trying to protect ourselves from them, we must become willing to see what they are revealing to us about ourselves in that same moment.* The difference between these two paths and their attending possibilities cannot be overstated. The latter leads to a revelation that the Divine already has a higher purpose for our life—one that includes all the powers we need to transcend any painful situation—while the former path ensures the fear and suffering that are inseparable from trying to protect the false images we have of ourselves, along with their imagined false purposes.

Yes, the path that leads to revelation is more difficult, but only in the beginning. Following its way, we are asked to look for the source of our suffering within us instead of what our suffering points to outside of us as being its cause. Why choose this route? Because it's only by deliberately illuminating these darkened corners of our own consciousness—where shadowy parts of us work in secret to misdirect us—that their authority over us can be brought to an end.

Author Vernon Howard always encouraged his students to choose in favor of this uphill path in spite of how challenging it may appear. His teaching on the subject was direct and perfectly clear to anyone weary of walking in circles. He always said when facing any difficult situation, including the darkness in oneself:

> *"Take the easy way and perpetuate the hard life; take the hard way and realize the easy life."*

Though it may seem too steep a hill to climb, especially the first time we consider its ascent, nevertheless, here's the first step that leads to freedom from useless suffering: *we must begin to doubt our own suffering*. To this idea the masses cry, "Impossible! Pain as real as ours is undeniable!"

No one is saying to deny this pain or to otherwise pretend it's not there. Yes, the feeling of any pain is real, but here's what we must come to see if we would set ourselves free: all the excuses we're handed—by ourselves—for why we must continue to hurt ourselves are like flies that travel with trash. The only purpose they serve is to make something worthless seem valuable; garbage is garbage, no matter how it comes wrapped!

Consider closely the twin truths in the following summary of this study. Within them rests the understanding—and the power—you need to start throwing useless suffering out the door:

- The justification of any negative state serves one end only: the protection and the preservation of the nature responsible for its manifestation.

- Any part of our nature that finds good reason to justify our pain is the source of that pain it justifies.

KEY LESSON

We are wrongly led to believe that life makes us into the kind of person we are. In truth, it's our level of understanding that makes life what it is for us! This is why nothing can really change for us until we see that trying to change some condition in life without first changing the consciousness responsible for its appearance is like blaming the mirror for what we don't like seeing in it!

Practice Makes Perfect

A well-respected pianist, Katherine had retired into a life of teaching. After more than twenty years playing in the city's philharmonic orchestra, her life was now dedicated to working with young prodigies so that they might fully realize the gifts with which they had been born. Her single wish was to pass along all the knowledge and skills that she had acquired over her many years as a master of the art.

One evening, following the first public recital of one of her most promising students, she asked him if they could share a word or two in private. Paul agreed, and after spending a few moments with friends and family to receive their congratulations, he walked into Katherine's small but well-appointed office. He had been in there before, but for some reason—maybe it was the tone of her voice when she asked to speak with him—he felt a little more nervous than usual.

"Please sit down," said Katherine.

"Thanks," said Paul. And even as he spoke the next words—"What's up?"—he knew they were far too casual, likely betraying his mounting apprehension that he wasn't there for a friendly conversation.

"How do you think you did this evening?"

"I don't know," Paul said, already realizing from her tone that she wasn't pleased with his performance. And to deflect the pressure he was feeling, he came back with a pretty quick response: "Everyone there seemed to think it was a good performance."

With no sign of a smile in her face, Katherine looked deeply into his eyes and said, "But I didn't ask you what *others* think of your work. I'm asking you...what's your opinion of how *you* played the piece we had prepared?"

At this point Paul knew that she knew and slumped ever so slightly in his chair. He had stumbled several times during the middle passages of the piece, and he had feared just that thing. The multiple, complex arpeggios in that section demanded a feat of dexterity only possible with the lightest of fingers; without this gentle touch, the emotional meaning of the entire passage was lost, so that the whole composition suffered accordingly.

With a sheepish smile, looking down at his feet, he said, "I know I didn't move well...at all...through the middle passages." And, after pausing a moment, he finished, "I'm sorry, Katherine. I really didn't mean to disappoint you."

"You're mistaken, Paul," she said. "My disappointment doesn't figure into this conversation. What matters is that you obviously didn't spend the time needed to prepare the piece. So, you see," she continued, "it isn't me that you've let down here...it's yourself."

"But that piece—that set of passages—is *so hard*," said Paul, looking up at his teacher, hoping for at least a little sympathy. But none was forthcoming.

"Answer me one question, Paul, and then I'll tell you why playing that piece seems as hard to you as it does."

"Sure...whatever," he said in a quiet voice.

"How much time did you put into practicing those sections? Be honest."

Realizing there was no point in pretending otherwise, Paul answered, "I didn't give it very much time."

Katherine called for his eyes with her own. "Exactly," she said. "And *that's why* it's so hard."

KEY LESSON

Once we realize that what makes any moment seem impassable is nothing other than our own resistance to what it asks of us, nothing remains impossible. Everything eventually yields to the one who persists.

Authority Over Whatever Punishes You

Whatever we try to go around in ourselves guarantees it will come around again, which is why the things we fear in life and about ourselves always tend to reappear. Here's the law that governs this relationship: whatever we resist in life persists as it does because *whatever we oppose grows!*

In the New Testament, Christ told his disciples, "Resist not evil." But when we translate this phrase from the Greek back into the original Aramaic language of the time, it reads as follows: "Do not oppose what opposes you."

Keeping the above new knowledge in mind, we can start seeing the wisdom hidden in other well-known spiritual laws, such as: "Judge not that ye be not judged." Our resistance to dark thoughts and feelings does not put distance between them and ourselves; just the opposite is true: our attention feeds them, strengthening their grip on us, which is why—just like being caught in quicksand—the more we struggle, the more we sink into the unwanted state from which we hope to escape. Nothing changes in such fights save for the arena in which we find ourselves pinned again by some recurring pain. It's time to walk an entirely new path—one that appears only in the light of the following higher self-knowledge:

Everything in the universe is created to change.

Nothing in existence is static; everything is always being acted upon by a trinity of forces whose celestial purpose is the revelation and perfection of all upon which they act. In exactly this same manner, what moves downward is designed to assist and help lift what moves upward; their connection is timeless, even though this invisible relationship is revealed only in passing time. And this grand theory of dynamic reconciliation applies directly to our negative states. They too exist and are created *for the purpose of being transformed into something else.*

Everything that appears within us, with no exception, is part of this beautiful process: transformation and transfiguration is the great law of life. In our physical world, the light of the sun—in any one of its infinite expressions—drives these changes. But what we've yet to understand is that this exact same principle holds true when it comes to any indwelling dark state. So now, let's bring this same higher understanding down into our everyday experience and see how it can help lift us above dark thoughts and feelings.

> *Any negative state that we choose to bring into the light of ourselves will be changed by that same awareness into which we bring it.*

This conscious choice—to be self-illuminating in the face of what seems to be dominating us—changes our relationship with the matrix of all that is real. Now life, its light, fights for us. Its authority cannot be challenged, which means that whatever we bring into its living light transfers this authority over to us. Dark states are now used for the higher purposes they are meant to serve, which, in turn, serves our true purpose in life, which is to be increasingly whole and free.

KEY LESSON

Nothing in reality is fixed; the illusion of some unwanted, unchanging nature within you is the work of unseen resistance to the ceaseless transformation that is the matrix of real life.

Find Peace and Quiet
in a Noisy World

Even though he'd only recently arrived at the secluded monastery, a young monk went to see the senior abbot. He took great care to explain how, no matter what he did to get away from noise, someone or something was disturbing the peace he had hoped to find there.

The wise old abbot listened, saying nothing. And when the young monk finished lodging his complaint, the two of them just sat there in silence, together, for about twenty minutes. Then the abbot broke the silence.

"Tell me of your mind, son; has it been quiet sitting here with me?"

The young monk squirmed under the question. He knew his mind had been nothing but a riot from the moment they had first sat down. "No, sir, it has not been quiet—not at all."

"I see," said the abbot, as he closed his eyes. Again they sat quietly.

The silence in the room grew painful, and before the young monk even knew he was talking, he could hear himself defending himself. "But master, surely my mind would more easily find its peace if things weren't so noisy here, wouldn't it?"

"Perhaps, perhaps..." said the abbot. "But not all is as it seems at first glance. For instance"—and he waved his arms around in a gentle circular motion, creating a small, cool breeze—"this air moving around us also carries with it the noise coming from the kitchen just down the hall." He paused to listen for a moment, then continued. "Can you not hear the noise of those who are preparing our afternoon meal?"

"Yes, I can, sir" he replied, glad that the abbot seemed to be taking his side.

"All of these different sounds travel through the air and, without the air to carry them, no noises would reach our ears to be heard, do you agree?"

The young monk nodded. The old abbot continued. "And yet the air itself is perfectly silent; its nature makes no noise." And he raised his eyebrows as if to ask yes or no.

Once again the young monk agreed.

With that, the old abbot stood up from the chair where he had been seated, indicating their time together was over. Smiling ever so gently, he said: "I trust you now understand the real source of what's disturbing you, but if not, let me make clear the truth of your condition: *nothing is louder than some noise you don't want to hear.* The real source of what disturbs your peace of mind is *not* this or that passing sound but your resistance to its appearance. You've yet to see it, but the noise stealing the stillness you seek is nothing but the sound of your own mind talking to itself about how to rid itself of its own noisy thoughts."

And just like that, the meeting was over. But as he walked back to his small room, the young monk knew that his quest to realize true stillness had now begun.

The sure way to guarantee that whatever's troubling you continues unabated is to keep talking to yourself about it!

Master the Twin Fires of Desire

There is an iconic passage in the New Testament attributed to Christ as he spoke to his disciples: "You can not serve two masters, for you will love one, and despise the other."

Taken on the surface of things, this quotation seems simple enough. But, like most of what Christ spoke, as is true for all avatars, the meaning of these words holds a far deeper esoteric meaning. In this instance, the "two masters" refers not to separate persons but rather to the nature of *desire*. Most of us assume that desire is the action of wanting something—a strong feeling of longing that wells up within us as a single force. But, as we're about to discover, any form of desire is the simultaneous appearance of opposing forces; terrible "twins" that are so closely bound together, they appear as one thing.

As an example, have you ever been somewhere and found yourself wanting to be someplace else? Or have you thought about yourself and then wished you could be someone else? We cannot desire to be someplace else without wishing we weren't in the place that we are; we can't wish to be someone else without wanting to no longer be who we are. As strange as it seems, *we want* and *we don't want* at the same time.

In moments like these we are the embodiment of opposing forces. Using a slightly different image, one side of desire pulls while its other side pushes away. We may not yet understand the nature of this push-pull creature and how one nature can embrace and resist life at the same time, but, with a closer look, we can see evidence of it all around and within us.

For instance, no one gets negative without first resisting the appearance of something unwanted. Perhaps we feel angry because something is not going as we imagined it would. We resist the event, seeing it as the cause of the conflict we feel growing inside of us. But what we're about to discover changes everything: the actual cause of our resistance, and its attending negativity, is hidden in our own desire.

We are not saying that there's anything wrong with desire—far from it; the nature of desire is instrumental in creation at all levels—but, like all things created, *it too is incomplete*. To desire anything *is to long for it*; the nature of anything that longs to be completed is obviously incomplete in itself. This helps explain, in part, why our desires burn on in the hope of a wholeness to come, spurring us to run after happiness as we do. But nothing that desire can imagine changes this one essential fact: no matter how many times it imagines and then builds a new foundation for itself, a house divided cannot stand. And there's still more to be seen about desire's divided nature.

Whatever desire runs after, that object of the heart or eye, means it's running away from something else at the same time! Experience proves this strange invisible fact. Hidden in the longing for fame or fortune is the hope of escaping some sense of fear or inadequacy. It would be helpful here if you were to think of your own real life examples. But here's the point: nothing that we are driven to acquire outside of us has the power to change this nature within us that sets us off and running.

Ask yourself: how many times have I won the object of my desire, only to find out that it wasn't enough? The prize won, whatever its name, didn't end the feeling we have of needing something else to make us feel whole and complete. So we enter another race, cross another finish line, and wait for the imagined peace or power we imagine as waiting for us there. But even if we get what we want, too soon we hear another starting gun go off, and off we go again! The question is: can we step out of this cycle and escape its secret compulsion? The answer is yes—providing two things: first, that we can see the truth in our findings up to this point, and second, that we're willing to continue our inner exploration. Assuming so, let's review before we go on.

Left to its own devices, desire cannot change the fact that whatever it wants or doesn't want is powerless to end its feeling of being incomplete. Whatever pleasure it wins or pain it manages to escape is always and only as momentary as being on a Ferris wheel, where being up means you're on the way down; it's inherent in the ride itself. Think how much this simple analogy explains about our lives. How familiar do the following statements seem to you?

"*This* is the greatest thing that's ever happened...but what if..."

"I love you...but..."

"This moment is *almost* perfect...all it needs is..."

It's almost as if something has to be not quite right before we feel as if all is the way it's "supposed" to be! This ever-present seed of dissatisfaction, the presence of a proverbial snake in the garden, seems unavoidable. And it is—until we realize desire itself can never lead us to the wholeness that *it* seeks. It can't. After all, how can something set against itself ever find happiness?

Releasing ourselves from our largely unconscious relationship with desire begins with learning to observe how it operates within us. No one can steal from us what we set ourselves to watch over, and the same holds true when it comes to the spirit of wholeness with which we are born. The only way we can be made to cling to some unhappiness is when we've been tricked into doing so. Use the wisdom of the following short rhyme anytime you start to feel negative; call on it to help you see through the sleight of hand that desire is using to drag you down:

The feel is real, but the why is a lie.

Of course we *feel* resistance to any unwanted moment; no one contests this, or that its attending pain isn't powerful, but now our eyes have been opened. We've seen that the "why" behind this negativity is an illusion: it is the dark byproduct of the opposing forces of desire. Let's look at a few more examples, just to be clear.

We can't get upset with traffic unless we've driven into that jam with an unconscious want. We don't see this psychic passenger until its pain is upon us; it lives in an unconscious desire that no one else be on the road when we are! The onset of this immediate resistance causes a constriction, and then comes its pain. Our immediate reaction to this pain is to escape the traffic we blame for it, but the traffic doesn't cause this pain; rather, it reveals the desire in which this potential pain always dwells. Still unaware of our actual condition, we rush to take whatever familiar escape route is offered to us: blame someone, break down, or break out of whatever we must to be free. Which brings us to the main point of this section: *we are being handed a "way out" of our pain by the same level of desire that created it in the first place!* As long as we ride this wheel of misfortune, we can do nothing but go round and round. What's the alternative? *We must learn to use this same moment of suffering to discover that this negativity is not ours!* As paradoxical as it may sound, no such unhappiness belongs to us unless we don't want it!

Resistance—not wanting something, anything—is a secret form of identifying with what is unwanted. This is why the more we struggle with not wanting, the stronger our attraction grows to what we don't want! Just ask anyone who tries to diet, give up smoking, or stay sober.

Think of the old Chinese straw finger puzzle. Once you put one finger from each hand in either side of the tube, the harder you pull in opposing directions trying to get free, the tighter grows the trap.

You are released the moment you realize the solution is to stop pulling. In exactly the same way, freedom from unwanted moments is no farther away from us than this unthinkable realization: *nothing real binds us*. Happiness and wholeness are not found on "the other side of the hill." The power to be inwardly content comes from learning how to stand on top of the hill, where all that we see—on both sides, at once—belongs to us. Let's review the principles we need to reach this next level.

We've learned that desire has a twin nature, that it is two masters in one; it wants and doesn't want at the same time. And because of this intrinsically divided state, it can't give itself the wholeness it longs for any more than one end of a pencil can embrace its opposing side. *Desire is incapable of transcending its own divided state of being.* Which brings us to this critical point in our study: if no set of opposing forces can transcend or integrate themselves, then the only thing that can reconcile and unite them is a third force.

The good news is that this unifying force already exists and always has. Depending on one's religion or spiritual inclination, this sublime Spirit of Reconciliation is known by many different names: the presence of God, the light of truth, Buddha nature, Christ, and many, many others. This celestial intelligence is not apart from anything that enters into it or into which it is invited. It serves all of life, and all serve its purpose, which is to unite all that lives, *including desire.* For our purposes, we will call this celestial character "higher awareness." And while we can't actually see this living light any more than we can see the light of the sun without the objects that serve to reveal it, we can look at how this new kind of awareness might work in a simple everyday example.

Imagine for a moment that you're out to eat with friends and someone makes an off-handed comment that everyone else laughs at, but that—for whatever reason—offends you. You can see that if the comment were truly as offensive as you feel it to be, then everyone there would feel it as inappropriate, which they don't. You can also understand that while the comment wasn't directed at anyone at the table, something in you feels certain the injustice was dealt to you alone. Either way, *what you don't want to feel* in that moment starts talking to you. It's telling you what to do and how to act to protect a part of you that insists no one ever speak out of turn, even though you're not sure what that really sounds like until it happens! In a heartbeat, your evening is ruined, and likely that of everyone else as well.

But now you understand how desire works against itself *and against you* whenever you're unaware of its limitations; you've seen that it can't want whatever it does—for instance, the approval of others—without fearing any moment in life where someone seems to mock or otherwise marginalize you. To have this new self-understanding within you is to have its light go before you...revealing this higher, truer path: instead of handing your attention over to what everything in you is pointing to as being the reason for your ruined evening, and then resisting and resenting it, you do something totally new: *you choose to be aware of what wants to defend itself in you instead of being tricked into defending it.*

You can make this new choice because at last you understand that any part of you that has a good reason why you should feel bad is not for you, but for itself! The clearer this revelation, the surer comes the following action: instead of agreeing to let it lead you nowhere, *you bring it into the light of your own higher awareness.*

Entering into this interior light changes everything about the moment because this higher level of awareness is *changing you from the inside out.* Your conscious agreement with this new order of awareness is the same as seeing the whole of yourself. All that was once hidden from your eyes now stands revealed—*including the parts of you that want and that don't want at the same time.* The dual nature of desire is at last reconciled, and you are released from its illusion. Standing there in this unifying light, there's no longer any need to look for a wholeness to come; *you are it.*

KEY LESSON

As long as desire remains unaware of itself, it can only chase its own reflection through time, always running after and reaching for something but unable to ever consummate the end of its own longing.

Step Out of the Flood of
Negative Thoughts and Feelings

Somewhere in a remote region of the Southwestern United States, a park ranger was seated in his high tower. It overlooked the deep canyons and ravines that ran through the national park where he'd worked for the past twenty years. Looking out over the terrain through his binoculars, he could see a thunderstorm gathering in the west and knew it was only a matter of minutes until a flash flood would come crashing through the canyons below.

Turning his extended gaze back to the east, something caught his eye. Less than a mile away he could see a young woman with a backpack just as she walked into one of the park's more well-known ravines, called "No Way Out." It was one of the most beautiful areas in the entire park because over the centuries innumerable flash floods had carved its sandstone walls into colored waves of red and yellow, as if the undulations of an ocean had been stopped in time.

A moment later, his mind put together the events happening at the opposite ends of the canyon. His heart began to race; there was no way this young woman could see the thunderstorm activity over the horizon just above her, let alone know that its storm waters were already pouring themselves into the other end of the narrow ravine she was exploring. He had seen countless such flash floods and witnessed their fury as they gathered everything in their way: boulders, brush, anything and everything—including any unfortunate creature caught in their raging waters. He knew she was doomed; it was clear the flash flood would likely reach her before he could possibly warn her of the danger. Nevertheless, he leapt to his feet, took the pole down to the tower floor, and jumped into his Jeep.

Less than three minutes later he pulled up to a spot on an open edge of the ravine where he knew he'd be able to see the woman below and hopefully shout out an alarm. He reasoned that if she had even a moment's warning, perhaps she might reach a ledge in the canyon and save herself that way. But, too late: he heard the waters coming even as he saw the woman round the blind corner and come face to face with their approach. He yelled, but the roar of the flood drowned out his voice even as he awaited the same fate for her.

The dark, debris-filled floodwaters were less than thirty yards away from the woman when she finally realized her situation. He could see the shock on her face, and he could imagine the terror she must be feeling. But instead of panicking and running, as he expected she might do, she seemed to go through some kind of shift. The next moment, as the raging waters closed within ten feet or so of where she stood, he could see she was saying something, talking to herself—perhaps a last prayer, he imagined.

He closed his eyes involuntarily, in part strengthening her prayer and partly because he didn't want to see what he knew was coming. When he looked again, the six-foot-high floodwaters had just reached her feet. Then came the inexplicable: instead of carrying her off with them, the surging waters parted before her. And as he continued to watch, she stood there perfectly still, just looking from side to side as if she was studying all the debris racing by.

"What on earth!" he thought out loud. Two minutes later, it was over. The waters had passed—only a trickle remained—and she was still standing there, bone dry. He shouted at the top of his lungs, "Wait right there! I'm coming to you!" Jumping in his Jeep, he reached her five minutes later.

"Please, by all that's holy, tell me what I just witnessed. Are you a magician of some kind? By all accounts, you should be dead. How are you still standing here?"

She smiled back at him. "Oh no, nothing like that," she said.

"Then what—what were you saying?" he fired back, a little surprised at his own agitated state. Quieting himself, he rephrased his question. "I could see you say something just before the floodwaters reached you. Was it a prayer of some sort? If so, please share it with me."

She paused, choosing her words carefully. "I suppose it is a sort of prayer. And I'm glad to share it with you if that's your wish."

"Oh yes," he said. "Please tell me."

"Well, when I came around the bend and saw the dark waters rushing towards me, I realized I had fallen asleep to my surroundings; there was no question I'd put myself in harm's way. So, after regaining my attention, I did the one thing that I knew was in my power to do."

The ranger could barely contain himself. Half sputtering his next words, he said, "Sure, sure … okay … but *what* did you say that caused the waters to part at your feet, leaving you there, safe and sound?"

She smiled. "All I said was *you go on without me.*"

KEY LESSON

Every flood begins with a single raindrop; the small streams they create become careening waters whose combined might washes away whatever stands in its path. All dark, destructive interior states begin with a single moment of unconsciously identifying with a negative reaction that soon turns into a torrent of tormenting thoughts and feelings. Your willingness to choose watchfulness over resistance to these surging states is the same as allowing them to pass by, leaving you safe and dry.

Realize Timeless Love

We have all been hurt, left with a heart wounded by others who seem to go on just fine without us. In moments of such loss, our emptiness doesn't stay empty for long; we are soon filled with anger, guilt, regret, or grief. These dark thoughts and feelings usually accomplish two things at once. At their onset, they bind us to a negative certainty that we will never again love or trust, but that's not the worst of it. They also blind us so that the real purpose behind our pain goes unseen; as such, we miss the following lesson. Hidden within it is the power to transform our tears into a new kind of triumph over sorrow:

It isn't love that has hurt us.

Once our inner eyes are open and we can read the story between the lines secreted away in our suffering, we're able to see one spiritual wonder after another. For instance, we realize that real love can't hurt us any more than the light from a lamp can turn a room dark. We understand without taking thought that the nature of light is to reveal, not conceal. It's clear: love heals; its celestial purpose is to integrate all that it embraces and all who choose to embrace it.

The birth of this new inner wisdom delivers the aspirant to a spiritual crossroads. The left-hand path leads to unrequited sorrow. The one on the right leads to revelation; from its elevated view, we see our heartaches—whatever their nature—as heralds of a higher order of love that bring a celestial invitation to realize a level of ourselves that cannot be diminished by any loss. The following insights bring these last important ideas into focus.

This world of ours, and all that transpires here, is a school for our spiritual education. Like any institution of higher learning, it has teachers, lessons, and many levels of learning; all serve to make possible the revelation and eventual realization of a timeless love that both creates and maintains the cosmos. Now, let's take the light of this same insight and shine it on that dark moment when life seems to take from us something or someone that we love.

Whenever we find ourselves hurt, left behind, or feeling undone by someone's negligent behavior toward us, life seems to be telling us that it's time to suffer. But this perception is as false as the lower level of self that falls for it. As we will see, the truth of these moments is far and away another story.

In any and all unwanted moments, life asks of us a single question: are we ready to see that our pain isn't because something has changed, as it obviously had to do, but rather we suffer because of a part of us that desperately fears change? As challenging as it may be, we must acknowledge this revelation if we wish to realize the lesson it brings. Only then can we take the true action for which this new understanding calls:

we must let go of any part of us that clings to its pain as proof of its love.

How can we be sure that letting go can help us outgrow our suffering, let alone learn to welcome those unwanted moments that seem to deliver us into its dark hands? A quick review reveals all:

Our own experiences have proven, time and time again, that the lessons we need in order to transcend our present level of understanding ride in on the back of events. Yet, in the midst of all these individual revelations lies hidden a single lesson greater than all of them combined: any truth that we come to see about ourselves is—and always has been—a part of our consciousness. Experience proves this divine discovery.

Whenever we finally learn the lesson in some moment and see the truth of it, the feeling is more like we've suddenly remembered something than one of having stumbled upon something formerly unknown to us. These moments of illumination are like running into a long-lost friend—and, in a way, that's what they are: the remembrance of any timeless truth reunites us with our immortal Self. We are led to these moments by a loving Intelligence that waits within us to show us that we have never been alone—and never will be.

This means that our life lessons appear as they do, when they do, to serve a beautiful single purpose: *to release us from the painful illusion that when something we love comes to an end, love itself comes to an end.*

What punishes us in these moments is our identification with a lower level of self that's trying to hold onto a form of love that can no longer be sustained in this world. This false nature suffers as it does for one reason only: it fears that the end of its relationship—with whatever it has become identified with—spells the end of its existence as well. And so it clings, denies, and decries all that passes because it believes that it's nothing without its designated "other."

Yes, it hurts to be left behind; there is always grief when a loved one passes on, as surely as we feel anger and sorrow upon learning that someone near and dear has betrayed or lied to us. This is why if we hope to realize the timeless love that lives within us, we must not only perfect the following understanding but also practice its truth in any moment where love seems lost:

In the worlds above us—that dwell within us—we are the other.

The indwelling love of the Divine never dies; it only assumes new ways to teach us this truth so that we may share in its ceaseless rebirth within us.

KEY LESSON

Anger or resentment toward someone who has left us does not prove we love and they don't. It proves we don't understand the true nature of love, or we wouldn't be ripping ourselves apart because someone tore from us something to which we had become attached. This momentary hole in our soul—created by such losses—must be left empty and not filled with negative states, otherwise we will never see the birth of a new and higher order of love within us because we've no room left for it to appear.

Everything Is
a Reminder of You

There's no way I could have known that every love in my life—every light through the trees, every song in my heart, every field in a breeze— everything bright and beautiful, kind, noble, and true is there to remind me of you.

The love we have for anything holy, beautiful, or true is present in our heart before we can think of any reason for the love that we feel. This means it isn't us who find things to love, but rather that Love finds—through us—a way to reach us and teach us that She lives in and through all things.

Put Yourself in
Heavenly Hands

There is a lower world where fears are real—where all things, and everyone living in this world, are unknowing participants in the fear that's found there. In this darker realm, *the thing feared is inseparable from the nature that fears it,* so that any action taken by this nature to end the fear it feels becomes the seed of its next fearful state.

For example, say that you're worried that someone you love may be losing interest in your affection. As this fear mounts, you start asking for emotional affirmation—seeking through words or by touch the attention you fear is waning. This push for consolation, created entirely by fear, produces exactly the opposite reaction in your partner, and he or she withdraws further. Most of us already know how this story plays out: in the end, we unwittingly cause the very thing we most feared would happen.

There is a higher world where fears such as these can't enter, let alone infect. Its peace is inseparable from its wholeness because in the higher worlds holiness is perfect protection; no creature can come into it that hasn't agreed to be one with its harmony. Any action taken by this nature is always in accord with the innumerable worlds in and around it; as such, these actions are the seeds of that peaceable kingdom from which they are sown. In the truest sense of the words, this world is the peace that passes all understanding.

It isn't so much that we live between these two worlds as it is that we're unaware of living in these two worlds at the same time. The world below knows nothing of the world above, while the world above understands everything about what dwells beneath it.

Knowledge alone of these inner domains does nothing to change your relationship with them, other than help make intellectually clear which of these two kingdoms should be the object of your soul's affection. About this there should be no confusion, any more than one would struggle to decide whether to collect sharp pebbles or precious pearls from the shoreline. However, just as it's true that discerning the difference between a smooth pebble and a precious pearl requires being able *to see* them, so is it true when it comes to knowing the difference between what is fearful or fearless within you.

This is why only the light of awareness of the entangled existence of these worlds can lead you safely through them and into the holiness that you seek. *This awareness is choice*, and this choice is action; together, they are one movement that serves a single divine purpose: to deliver you from out of the fearful hands of the lower worlds and into the loving hands of heaven.

KEY LESSON

In this world, a star is something you wish upon while hoping that your wish may come true. But in higher worlds—in the spiritual kingdom—your wish is your star.

Catching Messages from Heaven

Every relationship that we have in our life—our contact with each person, place, and event—serves a very special, if yet to be realized, purpose: it is a mirror that reveals things to us about ourselves that can be realized in no other way. I think this is one of the reasons that so many of us love to be out and about in that great showroom of life called Mother Nature.

For instance, gazing into the depths of a night sky we realize a sense of something vast and timeless; in her mountains we sense the soul of majesty; in any newborn there's a sense of an all but forgotten innocence. With all that touches us this way, we are made aware of a life larger than our own, yet one that is inseparable from the part of us that stands as witness to it.

Through these relationships we glimpse the ineffable; by their touch we are awakened to realize that whatever we behold in this world is but a mirror of the worlds above, and that all of these worlds reside within us. The soul knows this to be true: that in the common hides the celestial, and so it waits, watchful, never knowing when or where it will catch a message from heaven. Such moments are never announced. They enter quietly, unexpectedly, and—as the following illustration helps make clear—though they vanish into thin air, their impression lasts forever.

When autumn comes, particularly near its end, the ground on the little mountaintop where I live is literally golden brown with all of the oak leaves that have parted ways with their seasonal parents.

It's so beautiful to watch the thousands of leaves fall like slow-motion snowflakes finding their way to the forest floor and their temporary resting place there. Then come the late October–early November winds, and all the leaves are off to the races. Like a large gathering of tiny tumblers, they're driven here and there, rolling head over end in a dead heat to places unknown.

The remarkable thing I've always wondered about is where are they all going? Because even though everything is in movement, I can barely discern any difference in what remains before me. The leaves the wind picks up and scatters down the hill are replaced, moment by moment, with the leaves moving up the hill from the other side! It's something like a giant game of musical chairs, only there's a spot for all of the players. Slowly the lesson appears; a celestial secret is playing itself out right before me:

Everything moves, but nothing changes.

The ground over which these leaves race remains the same; it provides the stage upon which an infinite number of characters interact with one another yet never really change anything other than their places. This is a near perfect metaphor for any aspirant wishing to understand the relationship of their immortal Self with the world of passing time that runs through it.

Within us—at the very center of our being—is a spiritual ground, a perfect stillness that is to the movement of our thoughts and feelings as is the earth to the leaves that race across her until there's nowhere else to run. Resting from their race, they enter into her stillness, giving themselves up to nourish her body so that she may give birth again come the spring.

How can we better see this beautiful truth? What must we do to find the freedom that comes with realizing the changeless ground of the divinity that dwells within us?

Be here.

Be still.

Remember the truth of yourself.

By giving your complete attention to the living presence of all that you are, you will be given the incomparable awareness that while all around you everything changes, *within you lives what is unchanging.* Fearlessness follows this discovery in much the same way as late evening shadows flee the morning light.

KEY LESSON

What we call the present moment, including all that appears within it, is actually a timeless Presence; it is not the outcome of the past or a door to some imagined future. Passing time is just one of the ways in which what is always present appears, but this movement of time no more defines or confines this Presence than does the rising and setting of the sun change the nature of light.

End Your Fear of
Being "Nothing"

If the sky were empty, birds couldn't fly through it. The only way to know the fullness of the nothingness you fear is to *launch yourself into it.*

Do this enough times, and soon you will start to feel—and know—the presence of a timeless stillness that binds all things together. And though it touches nothing, and nothing touches it, still it connects all that moves through it.

In this vital "nothingness" lives everything, *including you.* This higher self-knowledge, once realized, ends the fear of being "nothing." Which means, at last, you've found something real!

You cannot protect yourself from psychological pain or disappointment and hope to court the Divine; awakening is a movement—a marriage of risk and revelation—that gives birth to a new order of being that is one with change.

Step Into the
Undying Self

As we're reminded in Ecclesiastes, "To everything there is a season." As each creation outlives its usefulness in one area of life, so does its purpose for being in existence change. For example, let's look at the life of a simple leaf. As it's born and slowly unfolds, it captures the soft light of spring and transfers this energy to the tree. Throughout the spring and summer, it serves this purpose. But come the fall, its service changes.

In its first birth, the leaf acts as an agent of conversion; it collects sunlight that, in turn, feeds the tree. But as the earth turns and fall moves into winter, the life of the leaf fades, dies, and drops to the earth. Its body is then slowly converted, becoming food for the same tree that it once helped to feed. And so the cycle of birth, death, and rebirth completes itself.

It's quite clear: no natural creature can escape the laws that necessitate its form and function being exchanged. And further, within this complex matrix of constant exchange is the total interdependence of all that play their part within it. Science confirms this fact: from massive suns to tiny mustard seeds, each and all, in the scale of their being, run through this cycle of life and death. In the end, the tree is as choiceless about its fate as are the leaves born from its branches. Our identification with the coming and going of all these individual forms keeps us from seeing the undying nature that hides behind them.

It should also be clear that less evolved creatures such as leaves, trees, and myriad beasts sheltering in their shade have no awareness of how their forms—after fulfilling one purpose in life—are obliged to transition from one order of being into yet another. They travel in and out of their various forms oblivious to the greater consciousness that they represent and are obligated to serve.

Yet, hidden somewhere in the complex matrix of our essence lies harbored a higher order of consciousness—a celestial level of being far greater than any temporary form it will ever assume. This transcendent self-awareness *remains changeless, true, and unflagging throughout time*. It never falters, even as it watches the temporary form it occupies "die"—pass on—so that this body can fulfill its next role in nature's designated plan. The awareness of this passage, which we alone are empowered to witness, has a name: it is called the dark night of the soul.

For those who aspire to know the immortal Self, the dark night of the soul is a required time of "unknowing." It marks a period of transition, a rite of passage that necessarily repeats itself each time we reach the end of an existing set of possibilities. During these tribulations there is no consoling ourselves—former pride and passion are seen as stumbling blocks, as pointless as they are powerless to rescue us from the self we now see they conspired to create in us. We are literally in-between worlds, suspended there by a supernal light showing us who and what we can no longer be, and yet not revealing what lies ahead should we surrender ourselves to its revelation. Here we enter into the proverbial valley of the shadow of death.

Yet, notwithstanding the fear of having reached the end of oneself, something abides with us in the midst of this spiritual darkness. It speaks to us personally through what it reveals to us about our present nature, which is why the longer we're willing to stand in the darkness of these light-induced revelations, the more surely do our eyes begin to see a secret inscription written there upon the heart. Part invocation and part invitation, its message is clear for all who have dared make it that far:

> *In times of great upheaval, if you will only agree to let go and die to yourself, it won't be you who passes. So that not only will you bear witness to the sacrifice of yourself, but you will also see your own rebirth.*

KEY LESSON

Our need to change—to be made new—is constant; however, so is our resistance to change. The former is inseparable from the freedom it heralds, while the latter ensures the continuation of patterns that imprison the soul. Choose the latter and living becomes dying, but choose the former and see how dying leads to life.

In Search of Perfect Spiritual Strength

The hardest part of the journey along the upward path is the gradual realization that our work to awaken to real life is, at best, imperfect. Along the ascending path, each footfall serves to echo an unwanted reminder of our imperfect actions, imperfect thoughts and feelings, imperfect devotion, and so forth and so on. However, seeing these image-shattering truths about ourselves is but half the trial and, in some ways, the lesser of the challenges to be faced along the way.

The greater part of this difficulty—and perhaps the most slippery part of the upper path—is the temptation to judge ourselves—to loath ourselves for whatever that "weakness" is that now sits exposed. The act of judging ourselves in times like these *seems* natural and even necessary if we hope to ever "outgrow" our own limitations as revealed. But this kind of self-laceration is a Trojan horse within whose dark recesses lies hidden a certain fact that, once perceived, frees us from the torment of self-judgment:

> *The pain in any unwanted revelation about our present level of self is created in that moment by the same low level of self that doesn't want to be revealed.*

Now, to this last fact add the following important idea: when our attention is drawn to how much we don't want to be what we are in that moment, we can't see ourselves as we actually are! This means that all forms of resistance-born reactions are blinding agents; they mask the fact of the moment with powerful, unwanted sensations that steal our attention so that instead of being self-aware—conscious of the whole of us—we are aware only of the painful reaction and what it points to as being the cause of our suffering.

Despising ourselves for missing the mark doesn't prove we could have hit the mark and didn't. It proves only that the unconscious nature involved in this kind of pain doesn't know what the true mark is or else it wouldn't be tearing into itself. This deception is as deep as it is cunning and dark: *hating ourselves for our weakness is the way secret weakness passes itself off as strength.*

Real spiritual strength is realized, slowly, by daring to detect and drop these blind negative states that we've been allowing to define us. And, believe it or not, this choice to no longer agree to ache over what you are not is the most difficult part of one's work to be free. After all, when there is no one and nothing left within oneself to blame for one's weakness, it's also pretty clear that turning to one's "self" for help is like asking a donkey for the directions to heaven.

The interior work to realize the immortal Self is a never-ending journey; and, contrary to popular belief, it doesn't begin with *our* wish to awaken but rather with God working *within us* to awaken us to the otherworldly nature of celestial love. If we agree to go through what is asked of us in this way, then it is through our union with the Divine—and the interior labor this calls for—that we gradually realize a conscious relationship with a love that is the same as life unending.

The time will come, if we persist, when we will no longer fear seeing our weakness but rather realize its presence *as a shadow that only appears as it does because of a living light that serves to reveal it.* And the greater this understanding grows, the greater the strength of this light becomes our own.

KEY LESSON

Seen through the eyes of higher self-knowledge, our weaknesses, whatever their nature, are the secret seeds of a new strength unlike anything imagined in our unending dream of overcoming what now defeats us.

Stop Feeling Empty

You wish and then rush to free yourself from fearful shadows but refuse to change the beliefs causing them, which is like jumping off the Ferris wheel onto the merry-go-round in the hopes of bringing an end to your dizziness.

Any attempt to bring an end to your sense of feeling empty serves only to strengthen the illusion of a false self that believes it can outrun its own imagined nothingness. Both illusions are filled with real enough terror, yet neither can be slain any more than a shadow can be put to death by a knife.

On the other hand, to allow emptiness its life—whenever it may appear—slays both the painful illusion of it as well as the false self that is so fearful of it. Then real Emptiness and her beautiful sister, Fullness, appear at the same time, revealing their timeless secret: they are celestial twins who are never apart from one another. They only seem to be separate from one another because each is so overwhelming to behold by herself that to look at just one blinds you to the existence of the other.

Within you—only still sleeping—lives a higher awareness that never fears the momentary appearance of any opposite within it.

Real love doesn't fear hatred any more than the sunlight worries over the shadows it helps to create. True strength is increased when a weakness it didn't know is revealed to it. To see and act upon these truths frees you from the fear of being empty or alone or in any other way unworthy of love.

The more you will step into the emptiness you fear, the sooner you will see that your immortal Self can never be empty any more than a sky without clouds is less than full.

The divided mind has but one love, and that is to divide life in two; nothing is sweeter to this unconscious level of self than creating the sensation of feeling apart from all that it sees. In this way it always has something to do because it never stops reaching for what it imagines it needs to make itself feel whole.

Jump Into the
Divine Wind

Life will fill whatever you empty—and whatever you fill, life will empty. That's the code—the higher understanding required for spiritual contentment all wrapped in mystery and filled with bittersweet contradiction.

It's all been spelled out once you learn to see. There's no sense in trying to save yourself by holding out. Besides, nothing you've managed to hold on to has yet filled that hole in your soul, has it? So, why fight the wind when you can join it?

Be as you're made to be: like a reed—hollow but whole. It's not just easier, it's much more profitable.

Then let the winds change their direction; it won't matter anymore which course they take because the more they play you, the more you get to play.

When you're wide open, everything blows your way. After all, nothing can shatter emptiness or steal its peace.

Offer yourself to the wind—and then jump in!

KEY LESSON

Our journey to the immortal Self commences with awakening to the timeless depth and breadth of our own sleeping consciousness. All that we are and hope to be already resides therein, waiting to reveal its light to whoever will dare make the leap into the seeming darkness of its perfect emptiness.

Divine Love Wants All of You

There are three ways to get what one wants from life: industry, cunning, or love. Industry is good but at best conditional, for it is subject to the passage and ravages of time.

The "crafty" inevitably trap themselves.

Love, on the other hand, liberates those who seek its company, and it is timeless. When all is said and done, this order of love has the last word because it is its own reward: whatever we are willing to let it make of us, it fashions from itself.

But communion with this timeless love has a cost. It asks for all that we are ... and more: it wants us *to want to give* what it asks of us. But real love never requests any form of sacrifice without first demonstrating why this magnitude of self-surrender is both wise and needed. And so it begins to prepare the heart for the road it's being asked to travel.

Slowly but surely, our eyes are opened to see the ruthlessness of passing time; we witness within ourselves—and in the lives of all that surround us—the inevitable sorrow born of identifying with the string of temporary loves that mark its passage. These revelations set the stage so that, before too long, what divine love asks of us becomes the one thing that we now want to give to it more than anything else.

What a mystery!

Now, for our willingness to give all, we realize that just the opposite has taken place: we've been given everything. We are being remade by love into what we were never able to make of ourselves: whole, happy, fearless, and free.

Your immortal Self is fearless because it lives for one reason only: to be the unflagging instrument—moment to moment—of whatever love asks it to be.

Find the Light in Your Darkest Hour

A pair of brothers set out for a day of extreme climbing on a mountain with steep rock faces and dangerous icefalls. They take nothing with them save for the gear they will need to enjoy an afternoon of climbing. But three hours into their ascent, they're caught off-guard by a totally unexpected storm of freezing sleet and hail.

Within minutes both men are near-hypothermic, and they realize that without shelter and a fire to warm them, they will not make it back down the mountain. So they dive into the first small cave they can reach.

Their brief search of the darkened space turns up some old pieces of wood, but even so, all of it seems hopelessly damp. By good fortune, they also find the remnants of an old, weathered backpack obviously abandoned there years ago. A quick examination of its contents provides nothing but some old candy bar wrappers, a camping knife, and a small piece of flint. They smile at each other. It's understood: their one hope lies in starting a fire, even though it seems against all odds.

Minutes later, they are taking turns; first one, then the other, striking the flint against a hard stone they took from the cave wall, hoping a spark will ignite a fire in the wood. But no flame appears—not even a trail of smoke to give them hope.

Before too long, the older of the two brothers despairs and gives up; he retreats into one of the cave's dark corners and, rolling himself up into a ball, wants only to fall into a sleep from which he is unlikely to awaken. But the younger brother remains steadfast; again and again he strikes the flint until his hands are torn and cut, barely able to hold onto the very tool he needs to save his life. Fifty times, a hundred times, a spark from the flint flies into the small pile of slivered wood and ... nothing happens.

Finally, his brother calls out to him from the corner where he lies. "What's the point, man? That wood's too wet; it will never ignite. C'mon, give it up, even if you don't want to. At least let me sleep in peace."

But the younger brother understands that unless he can create a flame, their lives are as good as over. So he says, "Look, you do what you have to, but I'm going to keep striking this flint to make a fire until either there's nothing left of it or I no longer have the strength to hold it in my hand."

Another hundred times he strikes the stones together. A hundred sparks fly straight into their wooden target, only to disappear into the darkness. Finally, he's so tired that he simply can't go on any longer. He has nothing left of himself or the flint. He looks down at the pile of slivers, his body gives a last shiver, and he passes out from exhaustion, sliding into the cold darkness that seems to be folding in all around him.

The next thing he knows, his eyes detect what seems to be a faint light flickering through their closed lids. And more—his face can feel something warm gently touching it! This thought passes through his mind: *what a sweet delusion—this must be the last thing a climber feels before he slips off into the abyss.* But instead of drifting back into the comfort of his dream, he makes himself open his eyes. And what does he see right before him? A small flame! His eyes open wide in disbelief: as impossible as it seems, a fire must have started when he struck his last blow!

Quickly but very carefully, so as not to put out the infant flame, he drops small pieces of wood into it. Gently he blows life into the growing, glowing, life-giving embers. Tense moments later, the dark cave dances with light and spreading warmth.

He gets up, walks over to where his brother sleeps, and awakens him with a soft touch, a smile, and a simple statement: "We're going to make it."

KEY LESSON

Whether to persist and aspire to the Higher or drop into some dark despair, that is the question; and which of these two seeds flowers all depends on which one you choose to nourish and grow.

Take the "High" Way Out
of Any Painful Confusion

Confusion is a kind of psychic traffic jam in the mind, often manifesting itself at the onset of some challenging moment. And while we usually blame this interior tangle on conditions outside of us, the facts—once revealed—tell another story.

Confusion is an inside job. It is caused by the simultaneous appearance of disparate, often conflicting thoughts and feelings all vying with each other for command of our mind and heart.

Picture a grid of roads with several cars in each lane coming from all four directions at once; all are backed up in the middle of a major intersection because the traffic lights have failed. As the pressure to get moving builds, each driver begins shouting to the others to get out of the way because he is sure how to get traffic moving again.

This illustration depicts well what happens within us whenever life asks us to take some action or understand some difficult situation and no clear route to do so appears at the same time. Almost instantly, different parts of us—each with distinct reasons for wanting what they do, and often in contradiction with one another—leap into the middle of the mental intersection and begin to fight with one another over the best way to untie the internal tie-up.

The key here to keeping yourself out of all such interior jams is to understand that none of these competing thoughts and feelings, and their attending strong sense of self, can undo the confusion you feel *because each one of these characters is secretly a part of it.*

The clearer you can see the truth of this interior condition, the easier it becomes to rise above it and pull yourself out of all that jam. Your reward is seeing that there's always another road waiting for you to take it—and that "high" way is always open.

*Lose Interest in the
Pain of Your Past*

There is no moment in which everything around us isn't beginning. In fact, if the various cosmos—from the greatest to the least—had a slogan, it would be this: *in with the new, out with the old.*

This celestial principle of regeneration is not only ceaseless in the world around us, *it is always at work within us, as well.* We are renewed every moment, from the inside out. Now let's see how this one truth can empower us to let go of any lingering pain of the past, whether from three seconds or thirty years ago.

We understand that the whole universe never stops changing and that we are each a part of this greater whole. Science confirms this finding; every cell in our body is exchanged within a period of seven years. No part of who we once were remains the same; every element is replaced with something new. These findings hold many self-liberating revelations, but none is more important than the following:

Since real life renews itself every microsecond, then whatever moment our mind keeps pointing to from our past can't possibly be *the real reason* for our present pain. We must look elsewhere for whatever stands between us and our right to be released from the pain of our past, which brings us to this:

Within us lives a lower nature that vigorously insists on remaining the same. While it would have us believe otherwise, this false self resists all that should and would naturally change within us. It clings tenaciously to images of past painful experiences that it has stored away even as it cries out, claiming that it can't escape their attending pain.

For example, perhaps we're having a morning cup of coffee at home or walking through a supermarket.

Our mind is mingling with all the available impressions, and merrily we float along in their stream. And then, unbidden, comes a certain thought, triggered perhaps by an image or familiar-looking person that catches our eye. In a flash, though virtually unconscious to us, that impression triggers a string of associations with some old, emotion-laden image from our past. The next thing we know is that we're knee-deep in a struggle to escape the suffering of that negative memory. But what we can't see in this same moment, and that we need to, is this: *the part of us wrestling with that pain from our past is a very familiar sense of self that can't exist without the past it says it can't stand!* As the famous cartoon character Pogo once said, "We have met the enemy, and he is us!"

Our knowledge and awareness of this unconscious nature is the key to our power over it whenever it attempts to deceive us into reliving *its* life. The clearer the following new understanding becomes, the nearer we are to the freedom it brings: *this lower level of self must have something to resist in order to exist.*

This false nature has no power of its own; whatever strength it has to cause us suffering, it must borrow from us. The decision *not* to push away this pain—or, for that matter, to do anything at all about the past upon which it is blamed—is within us. Ours is the power to give this pain, and the level of self responsible for it, *nothing* but our awareness that the time has come for it to be made into something new.

KEY LESSON

Any painful past moment must pass
the moment you lose interest in it! Stop
looking at what you don't want to see,
and soon you'll see it no longer.

A *Sure Prescription for a Profitable Spiritual Life*

Long ago, an illuminated teacher of truth called his small group of students to his side. He smiled gently and then went on to tell them that the day had come for him to depart this world.

After quieting their fears that they would be left without guidance, he assured them they would never be alone in their quest for real life as long as they put their love for truth before all else. And then, without further ceremony, he stood up and turned to leave the room.

As all eyes watched him walk away, the teacher had just about reached the door when he suddenly came to a stop; it was as if he had remembered something important. A moment later, he reached into his small leather bag and pulled from it a handful of handwritten papers, all the same size. He then walked around the room, handing each student his or her own copy. When he was done, he turned to face them all. These were the last words they were ever to hear their beloved teacher speak out loud.

"To ensure your progress is sure and steady on the upper path, I've taken the time to write out for you what I know is a perfect prescription to ensure that each of you have a profitable spiritual life." He paused for a moment, taking time to make direct eye contact with each of them. He then continued.

"What I want you to know is that while this medicine is strong—especially at first—it has great power to set straight all that remains misguided within you! So I want all of you to give me your word that you will follow this prescription until you are whole and free."

A silence fell over the room until one young woman spoke: "You have my word." And then came a chorus of consenting voices. The old teacher smiled again, turned, and was gone.

The following five lessons are the prescription he left them that day. Insights such as these, and their implied instruction, are rarely discussed among the spiritually uninitiated because of the measurable disturbance that their strong medicine causes in the soul. Nevertheless, welcome these truths into your mind and watch how their refreshing view of reality leads you to that unconditional freedom for which your heart longs.

- To weigh the value of what this world can
  reward us with, we need only remove the
  scales from our eyes, for were we willing
  to measure how many times we have
  fallen victim to a world that promises us
  victory but that leaves us a victim, then we
  would know just how hollow is the hope
  of finding treasure in a bottomless basket.

- If common social convention—with all
  its contrivance and hypocrisy—has one
  redeeming value, it is this: the happy day

may come when we realize that too much of our time has been spent conversing with cleverly disguised thieves, listening to and believing in the plans of liars, and trusting in the promises of people who are, by majority, incapable of a single act of integrity. This day of our awakening is the same as the delightful date of our departure from a bankrupt world filled with beggars dressed as kings and queens.

- Billions give their lives away for a moment's pleasure or the promise of approval. They sacrifice their happiness in the hope that by acquiring power they can make their world a prettier place in the face of all the ugliness that these same pursuits create. The few and the true also give their lives away—in acts of quiet selflessness that naturally follow the footsteps of those who have preceded them on the upward path.

- For anyone with ears to hear, there is
  but one question and one answer: will
  we wait patiently for a single moment
  of relationship with what is eternal and
  real—where, with the touch of something
  timeless, all the moments of our life are
  forever changed? Otherwise we waste
  the few moments of our life chasing the
  pleasure of an imagined time to come that
  forever recedes from our grasp in the same
  instant that we reach for it.

- No one can say no to this world who
  is afraid to walk through it alone. The
  unseen cost of this baseless fear is not just
  ending up in the company of cowards
  but that one may lose the possibility of
  ever coming to know the company of the
  Divine.

KEY LESSON

*Until the peace and pleasure found within
yourself is equal to or greater than any
consolation found outside of yourself, then
your power to be patient, loving, and profitable
in every moment is, at best, conditional.
Nothing better serves to sustain anger,
frustration, and fear than being identified with
a level of self whose life is founded, at best,
upon the sands of passing circumstances.*

*Six Ways to Know a False Inner
Guide from the True One*

As we've already pointed out, the journey to the divinity within has its dangers. About this we are clear: the inner path is lined with many trials and pitfalls. But there is nothing to be feared in this foreknowledge; in truth, these encounters are actually stages of initiation; they are necessary points along the upper path where the aspirant reaches—again and again—the proverbial fork in the road.

A great confusion usually clouds these unwanted moments, made all the worse by yet another challenge that is, itself, a part of the path less taken: the

aspirant can't see down either path, as a kind of darkness shrouds the entrance to both.

It is always in these moments that the aspirant
feels most frightened and alone. A mounting despair
strengthens the sense of fatigue; an outpouring of
stressful thoughts and worried feelings deny, decry,
and try to console all at once. But the main question
remains, which we'll put in the first person:

How can I tell which of the two paths is the true
one? Which leads to the immortal Self, and which is
a one-way ticket back to being "me" again? And how
do I know which—if any—of these voices in my head
telling me "*this* is the way" or "*no*, go that way" is
offering me the right instruction? In short, how can
I tell the difference between a true inner guide and a
false one?

Is there a way to know with some certainty which
of these guides can see through this darkness and
which one is blinded by it? The answer is yes.

The following six ways are designed to help you
tell the difference between a false inner guide and a
true one. Use the light these insights provide to help

you make it, safe and sound, all the way back home to your immortal Self.

- The true inner guide fears no outcome, while the false inner guide can't stop trying to protect itself from its own imagined fears.

- The true inner guide quietly invites you to take a new direction, while the false inner guide first pressures and then pushes you in the direction that it wants you to take.

- The true inner guide is unshakable, collected, and composed, while the false inner guide is always on the verge of coming unglued.

- The true inner guide never tries to talk you into an action, while the false inner guide can't stop talking about the action it wants you to take.

- The true inner guide understands that you must make mistakes along the way, while the false inner guide harshly judges every misstep.

- The true inner guide remains open and receptive to any life lesson, no matter how unwanted, while the false inner guide shuts down and rejects any revelation that threatens its flattering self-image.

KEY LESSON

Nothing infuriates evil as much as being seen for what it is.

The Secret Garden of the Soul

Much as we might find ourselves on a hillside watching helplessly as an approaching storm overtakes where we stand, there are times when we know a sorrow is coming but are unable to get out from beneath its pain.

Sorrow that not only didn't we tell someone of our love for him or her, but sorrow also that we couldn't speak the truth of our heart—or that we just wouldn't—for fear of being misunderstood.

Sorrow that we didn't take a much firmer interior stand against what we could see defiled our soul, or sorrow that when we did attempt to be strong, all we found was the depths of our own inadequacy.

Sorrow over wasting so many precious hours pleasuring ourselves with meaningless pursuits, and sorrow for the fact that we knew better but feared emptiness more than regret.

In these observations there is no joy—only a faint sensing, a dim realization, that for these revelations something within us *must* die; further, that the deeper run its roots, the more meaningful will be its passing...

If we will stand there in these seemingly dark moments, one thing becomes increasingly evident: the growth of our soul rarely unfolds in a light that we recognize as such. Many times, darkness is the medium, sorrow the seed, and the subsequent humility conceived in these trials is the divine garden in which our soul flowers.

KEY LESSON

*It is through our awareness of imperfection—
of seeing our own shadow appear, spread,
and then falter in a supernal light—that the
Divine first gives us a glimpse of its eternal
perfection and then invites us to enter.*

It's All or Nothing

What drives us mad isn't the opposing actions of life or the erratic behavior of someone close to us. The source of our craziness is an inside job. Our mind is divided; it is a house set against itself in the truest sense of the words. A few simple examples more than prove this assertion.

Whatever one part of us is for, another part usually stands against, ensuring some kind of painful debate. For instance, most of the pleasures we take are accompanied by a torment that we ought not give in so easily to that desire.

Whenever we face some challenging circumstance, we rarely choose a choice of action without first being brought into a court of appeals. Every possible thought and feeling takes the stand, some for and some against what we intend to do. Then, after being prosecuted by the fear of making a bad decision, we "decide" to postpone what needs to be done, even though this procrastination is as punishing as the fear from which it springs.

False beliefs and socially conditioned, culturally corrupted morals go before us like a battering ram, running headlong into anyone or anything that doesn't think like we do. There is mistrust, even enmity, toward those who love any god besides our own, and this self-punishing fear and anger is justified by calling others ignorant.

Even when we suspect there may be a sickness in our soul, our solution is piecemeal: we look the other way by donating time or money to those "less fortunate," promising to meditate or exercise more, or joining some organization promising to make the world a better place. These half-hearted actions give rise to half-results: sorrow and suffering remain in place. Nothing real changes because we don't.

We cannot change ourselves by actions in fractions any more than we can change soured milk by removing one curd at a time or by adding fresh milk to it in increments. Either the whole of us changes or not; our being is not its individual parts but the sum of sun and earth. It really is all or nothing.

KEY LESSON

True spiritual progress is inseparable from seeing and agreeing to undergo whatever these revelations make evident must now change in our character. Such divine interaction never moves in a single direction but rather occurs in all directions at once, like the radiations of the sun. This order of light doesn't transform the darkness into which it enters; it exchanges it with its own celestial character.

Stop Trying to Make
Something from Nothing

If you serve only yourself, you serve nothing.

If you cling only to yourself, you hold nothing.

If you hunger for the approval of others, you starve for nothing.

If you wish to please only yourself, you please nothing.

If you have only possessions as pleasures, you have nothing.

If you strive to amass only wealth, you count for nothing.

If you are wise only in the ways of this world, you have learned nothing.

If your heart beats only for yourself, you live for nothing.

KEY LESSON

The sorrow and emptiness of any self-centered existence springs from ignorance of the immortal Self; it is to live from a compulsive and fearful nature that can never quite satisfy its hunger for more, regardless the cost to all who suffer for its appetite.

The Key to Spiritual Freedom

Sometime early in the fifth century, a small fishing boat ran into a sudden unexpected squall. The storm shattered its mast and, without a sail, it soon drifted out of familiar waters and into the sea of a neighboring but hostile country.

A week later, the poor fisherman was captured by the captain of a foreign ocean-going vessel where, alongside dozens of other slaves chained to their oars on either side of the ship, he was forced to row merchants and dignitaries to their given destinations. It seemed his fate was sealed: he would have to spend the rest of his life a captive, enduring unspeakable hardship and deprivation.

But this man was unlike any of the other poor souls on the ship. While they would cry, "Why did this happen to me?" our hero refused to lament his situation. And when they talked about what their life used to be like—how they once had a good home, family, fine food and wine—he refused to think about the past or reimagine its pleasures.

Rather than use his time resenting or reliving his life, he spent all his time carving a wooden key out of a little chunk of broken oar. And since there were no tools, he used his own shackles to do the shaping. Every moment when he wasn't rowing, his interest was in making the key that he hoped would open his shackles.

Now everyone knew that the old iron lock on his shackles was probably rusted solid, especially after not having been opened in several years. No metal key was likely to turn it, let alone a wooden key! And so the fisherman was the laughingstock of the ship because his free time was spent trying to make a key that would never unlock anything. But the improbability of his situation was his last concern. He wanted only to do what was in his power while refusing to do what was not, which was to change his immediate circumstances.

After a while, one of the guards—who couldn't help but admire the fisherman's persistence—even drilled a hole in the top of the key for him. Then he gave him a piece of leather cordage to put through it so that he might wear the key around his neck. And so it was; day in and day out, the old fisherman continued working on his key.

Years later, a nobleman who was being ferried on the ship asked if he could go see for himself the conditions below deck. As he walked down the stairs, he spied the fisherman wearing a beautiful key, which by now was intricately carved and burnished by time. The nobleman pointed to it and asked, "Where did you get that beautiful key?"

"I made it."

"From what?" asked the nobleman.

"I used my shackles to carve it from a broken piece of oar."

Something about this slave intrigued him, and so the nobleman came to hear the story of how the fisherman fell into his unfortunate situation as a slave.

Returning to the upper deck, the nobleman went straight to the captain. "I wish for you to release the man with the wood key around his neck to my keeping. I recently lost my best carpenter, and I want this slave to return home with me to become my household craftsman."

Moments later a deal was struck, the cost paid, and within that same week the fisherman found himself in a new home.

Even though the wooden key he carved never opened the lock that bound him to his chains, *it still won him his freedom*. He became a beloved, highly valued member of the nobleman's household. Many years of faithful service later, he was set free to return to the home of his birth.

KEY LESSON

The wise, finding themselves adrift at sea, are ever watchful for a favorable wind to come and fill their sails. But, while they wait, they row night and day on the heading they believe will lead them back to the safety of their home shores.

Your Role in the Revelation
of the Immortal Self

Distinct moments come along the upper path when it feels as if a dam has burst in one's heart; wild waters of unknown emotions race into and through the canyons and once-sealed chambers of consciousness, washing clean all that has come before. Everything trembles in their passing. The mind races as well, but more for its uncertainty than in accord; it seeks to contain these forces before they can carry away its reason.

These innermost stirrings are the sometimes frightening effect of the soul's awakening, where each breath it draws reveals the presence of unimaginable influences and latent powers beyond the aspirant's ability to control. But the movement of these celestial forces must not be dampened simply because we've yet to understand the purpose of their presence within us. They are not asking us to know what they want; these forces are self-organizing.

They race and swirl and disrupt and digest all in their path because they are building something anew from themselves within us, so that we must turn them loose—we must let go of what we might hope to extract from them and, instead, allow them to exact their celestial influences upon our soul.

These energies are the new blood: they are stirrings of spirit that speak to us in wild pulsations whose origins are the stars. We cannot know their native language any more than our physical ears can hear the intelligence inherent in the light of awareness, which is why we must allow their impressions to assemble within us without interference.

They seek to build a new universe of infinite individual galaxies; and we—each of us—are the matrix, star stuff, and deep space created for their celestial nurturing if we will agree to our part in this divine revelation of the immortal Self.

Just as all the qualities of the ocean can be found in a single drop of its water, so do all the infinite expressions of consciousness— high and low, light and dark—dwell within our heart, mind, and soul.

Open the Door of Your Heart to the Divine

There was once a woman who, longing to make a new start after a painful divorce, moved with her young daughter to a new town. Part of her plan included opening a small shop in the town's main square that would feature beautiful and unique objects from all around the world.

Several months later, the big day arrived. The shop was brimming with all the things she loved. Tea and cakes were set out on silver trays; everything was ready. And so she eagerly awaited all the customers she expected to come pouring in; but, as the morning passed, not a soul walked through the door. She began to despair.

Later still, with the day drawing to a close and without a single customer having come into her shop, she could no longer contain her dismay; she finally let out a deep sigh, followed by a complaint that she couldn't help but speak out loud.

"Where is everyone? How is it possible that no one cares enough to even drop in and at least say hello? Is it even possible that the things I love so much could mean so little to everyone else?"

Overhearing what her mother had said, her daughter lifted her head from out of her coloring book and said, "But Mom, of course no one has come in; what did you expect?"

The mother looked at her child with an expression that said *what—are you kidding me? Like you know what the problem is?*

And dropping her head back into the coloring book, her daughter said, quite matter-of-factly, "Well, just thought you'd like to know—you never put your Open—Please Come In sign on the door!"

KEY LESSON

*Is it better to know or not know the truth
of oneself in any given moment? To answer
this question in the affirmative—and to then
respond accordingly—is to fling open the doors
of perception, welcoming into your heart the
divine light that alone can make you whole.*

A Short Commentary on
Conscious Suffering

Brooding, resenting, blaming, regretting—all are forms of unconscious suffering; each and all serve to strengthen the false notion that our negative state is caused by a condition outside of us. These dark shadows that always trail behind unwanted moments serve a distinct purpose. Their job is to create, and then support, the impression that we have just been made into a victim of circumstance.

Once we embrace this false perception, the pain of not wanting things to be as they are gains the upper hand; as our resistance grows, so does our spiritual blindness. Before long, it's almost impossible to see the truth of our actual condition, which is exactly what the false self set out to achieve. This lower nature lives, literally, to keep us from seeing that our experience of life *is a reflection of our present level of consciousness*.

Suffering over *any* false perception is worse than useless. First, it strengthens the illusion that forces exist greater than our divine right to transform them into something useful for the development our soul. But this same level of unconscious suffering supports another false conclusion: that we have no choice but to surrender ourselves to what *it tells us is true about ourselves*. And that's where the timeless idea of conscious suffering comes into play.

To suffer consciously is to act in a whole new way when faced with the appearance of any unwanted moment: instead of mechanically resisting the situation, along with the painful sense of self that appears with it, we take another path—we choose to be *consciously passive* to these negative states that are actively blaming or judging. In this way, rather than being made into the unwitting instrument of these dark radiations, it is we who act by bringing the light of awareness into and upon them.

This new action of being quietly passive to painful thoughts and feelings is conscious suffering. In its abidance, one dies to the nature of what is falsely active by aligning oneself with the true action of a living light that changes whatever is brought into its healing wholeness.

KEY LESSON

Whoever doesn't know himself unwillingly suffers for the sake of ignorance. Whoever works to know himself agrees to suffer for the sake of wisdom. Whoever becomes wise slays the suffering born of ignorance. And whoever transcends the suffering born of ignorance shares in the birth and burden of creation, in which can be found no greater peace or joy.

Take Time to Be Alone

Your heart needs space to soar. Your mind needs places without walls to wander and time by itself to see its own reflection.

Give them this gift, and they will bring back to you the freedom they find, filled to the brim with bright new possibilities.

Be patient with yourself.

It takes practice to perfect doing nothing—not that this work isn't native to your soul, only that so much of us is so busy trying to be something, we have become distracted and have forgotten being whole.

So take time to be alone. Feel everything, but be no one. Dip yourself in this nothingness. Throw yourself in, and then listen to the sound of no bottom.

And do not fear such aloneness. What you call falling *is flying*—once you let go of being afraid.

KEY LESSON

Once living within the limits of what is known is also realized as being the limitation of your spiritual possibilities, then there is no recourse other than to depart the safety of all that you have been in favor of discovering all that you are yet to be.

An Invitation to Outgrow Your Limitations

Have you ever noticed how the more negative you get, the more difficult everything about your life becomes, including being able to do the simplest things? It's like suddenly sinking into dark molasses, where not only can't you move, but everything you don't want seems stuck to you!

To the spiritually uninitiated, it feels as if you've been dropped into a river of resistance but, in truth, *you are being pulled into it by a lower level of self that wants you to look at whatever challenges you in life as an adversary.* Its attempt at deception—to negatively alter your perception—is the only power it has to keep you from seeing unwanted moments as they are in reality: an invitation from the Divine to outgrow your present limitations. Regardless of the nature of the trial set before you, it asks, "Would you like to live in a larger world—one without fear? Do you want to be less worried or angry and more at peace with yourself?"

We may not yet be able to hear these questions or discern for ourselves the perfect timing of their compassionate appearance, but they are always present at the "point of impact"—whenever some event reveals an unseen limitation of ours. We may be given to see, for instance, how our impatience with someone we love trumps our wish to be more understanding of him or her, or perhaps we see that anger still gets the best of us when pressed into some stressful situation. You fill in the condition, but here's the point:

No unwanted condition or its outcome can change until we outgrow the nature responsible for it.

This realization empowers you to do something with unwanted moments that has been impossible before. Now, instead of trying to avoid those moments of crisis where you feel suddenly inadequate or limited in some way, you see—and meet—these old fears as a new opportunity to realize the boundary line between who you have been and are yet to be. All seemingly impassable moments in your life are seen for what they are: a predestined place for you to meet, let go, and outgrow that lower level of yourself that used to stand fearfully before it. The boundary between limitation and limitless disappears, and now *you stand on the side of unlimited possibility.*

Freedom is not found by fighting with what you think stands in your way; your true spiritual liberation rests within this one unthinkable realization:

What is in your way is part of the way.

Once it's understood that whatever seems to be set against you has actually been put there for you to outgrow it, then you have received, opened, and accepted the invitation of the Divine. The rest is done for you.

KEY LESSON

*In many ways, the true blessings of life often
come disguised as the worst moments, but
those who will patiently bear the presence
of that emptiness—of what seems to be a loss
or painful limitation of some kind—will
soon see its temporary mask fall away and
witness there, in its place, the appearance
of an impossibly kind and loving face.*

Be United with Your Immortal Self by Saying "I Do"

A great king sent out a declaration announcing a contest for an unimaginable prize: an irrevocable share of the kingdom itself, including all of its riches. The rules for the competition were simple: all citizens had to offer the king something nearest and dearest to their heart, and the gift that pleased him above all the rest would determine who won.

When the appointed hour for the contest finally arrived, all the citizens assembled in the castle's great hall. The excitement was palpable. They were told—upon being invited to step forward—that each person should approach the throne and offer their gift. Once the presentation was complete, they were instructed to step to the right side of the throne and stand there directly underneath a beautiful golden crown that seemed magically suspended in the air. It was explained that the crown would descend by itself to rest upon the head of the one whom the king chose as having offered the greatest gift.

The ceremony went on for hours. Everything from rolls of silk, treasure chests of various sizes, family heirlooms, and bottles of home-pressed oils and wine were spread out before the king. Some of the nobles promised the wisdom of their counsel or the services of their personal guard. But to everyone's dismay—a general discontent that grew greater as the day turned into night—at no time did the golden crown descend from its suspended place to grace a winner.

At last there was only one man left in the throng of citizens who had yet to approach the king. He was known by his friends to be of little means, a simple man who owned a small vineyard of no particular account.

When the king summoned him to come forward, Christian stepped out from amongst the crowd. A few laughs, obviously contentious, were heard above the growing murmurings of the crowd. Surely Christian had to be the last person on earth worthy of a share of the kingdom.

He walked quietly up to the throne, briefly looking into the eyes of the king, and lay at his feet what looked like—from the vantage point of all who were watching—a simple letter. But rather than stepping beneath the golden crown, Christian excused himself and began walking out of the hall.

As the King opened the letter to read it, more voices sounded out of the crowd, some openly deriding Christian's meager gift, others challenging the king's process of selecting a winner. Amongst all the bother, no one noticed the smile that had come over the king's face. The next moment, the king spoke for the first time. He called to Christian, saying, "Young man, come back; you have yet to stand beneath the golden crown."

Christian said nothing as he walked back towards the king's throne and where the crown sat suspended in the air next to it. A few snickers could be heard coming from the crowd. Someone in the back, unseen, shouted out, "Oh sure, like he has a chance!" And that prompted other discontented voices: "Let's get on with choosing the winner!"

At just that point, as instructed by the king, Christian stepped beneath the golden crown. Scarcely a heartbeat later, the crown started to glow. Another moment passed and from the center of the crown a bright shaft of conical white light came down over Christian, encircling him from head to toe. Then, as everyone stared in disbelief, the golden crown descended to softly rest upon his head.

No one made a sound; no one moved. A stunned hush filled the great hall. And then—from somewhere out of the crowd—someone shouted out, "What's going on here?"

Another voice chimed in, challenging, "Why him?" Soon others were sounding their similar complaint.

The king rose from his throne and walked over to where Christian was standing, and then he raised both of his hands, quieting and addressing the mob at the same time: "Are you sure you want to know the answer to your questions?"

Slowly but in growing intensity, a chorus of voices made known its wish: "Yes!"

"Then, with your patience, I shall tell you"—and with that he took Christian's letter into his hand and began reading it out loud:

"My dear king, how I wish this letter offered you whatever you had hoped to receive from one of your profitable citizens. Never before have I wished for anything more than for a share of your kingdom. So much so that when I first heard about the contest, I had the thought to misrepresent myself and my possessions; I wanted to seem—before you and all gathered here—an invaluable, indispensable person. But before too long the whole idea of such a pretense became too painful to consider. In the end, knowing how the contest stated everyone must present you with something, I decided to write this letter. The fact is I have nothing of my own that might warrant being awarded the prize offered here today, but I think you already know this.

"Like everyone else in your kingdom, whatever I have, you gave to me: you provided a home in which to live, a field to plant, even the seeds I used to make whatever profit I could; all of this was given to me freely. So what can I possibly offer you that isn't *already* yours?

"As for promising you some skill or power of mine—as I imagine many of my peers will do to curry your favor—all I can tell you is that I have none of these things, at least not in the way I once imagined.

"I have come to see because of the kind of light that permeates every corner of your kingdom that none of the qualities upon which I once prided myself are what they seem to be.

"For instance, I have seen that my anger, which often feels so righteous, or my unfailing ability to instantly judge others proves neither the strength nor the wisdom of the character enacting these states; far from it. It's clear that the only thing served by blame is a lower level of myself that points out the faults of others in order to keep itself from being seen. Now I see these acts of aggression for what they have always been: weakness pouncing on weakness.

"As for being a giving, caring person, I know I may have fooled others in the past, but I am no longer able to fool myself. When push comes to shove— as it always seems to do in this life—my first interest is to protect myself. Of course some say, 'This is how it's meant to be.' It seems truer to my mind that this popular convention simply masks our actions when compassion or love proves to be inconvenient.

"I could go on, but to be clear: the only thing— other than this letter—I have to give you is my everlasting gratitude for the place you've given me in your kingdom and all that living here has made possible for me to see."

The king carefully folded Christian's letter into his robe and began speaking directly to him.

"You, above all these others, have brought me what my heart treasures above all else; my greatest joy is to exchange it for the keys to my kingdom. Do you know what this one thing is that you have brought here today, that none other has offered me?"

Christian, still unsure over what was going on, answered no.

And the king said, "*Humility*—the one thing that he who bears it would never consider a gift, let alone worthy of giving to a king."

"I ... I don't understand," said Christian.

"Nor would I expect you to at this point along the path," says the king. "However, that you might better understand, I will tell you something more.

"*Humility* is the crowning of the soul. Much as a wildflower blooms after the touch of summer sun, only the heart opened to humility can be transfigured into an instrument of love. And this love born of true humility is conceived in only one way: through a single selfless act. Do you know what that act is, Christian?"

"No, Your Majesty, I do not."

The king smiled to himself, apparently amused by his own thought. "It all happens each time a daring soul such as yourself says *I do* to that divine question asked of everyone in the darkness of an unwanted moment:

"*Will you accept the truth about yourself that my light has come to reveal to you? Because if you will say*

"I do"—and bring me into your life—I will bring you into mine at the same time.

"'And when our spirit has become as one, you will never again fear, fight with, or stand in judgment of anything you see. This is the gift of humility: to know, without taking thought, that whatever you are given to see by my light is now and always has been a part of your immortal Self.'"

KEY LESSON

Just as a caterpillar can't possibly understand the unique forces acting upon it serving to transform its earthbound body into an airborne butterfly, neither can our lower self know anything about the living light that transfigures whomsoever will agree to stand within it until its work is done.

How to Never Forget the One You Love Most of All

H e had come upstairs and into his young daughter's room for a distinct purpose: over the last few months, he'd been watching as she had let her room—in particular, her collection of stuffed animals—run wild.

Standing there, surveying the piles of cuddly creatures that were thrown around the room and that overflowed her toy chest, he looked at her as if to say *really?* She got the message. "I'm sorry, Daddy," she said. "I'll put everything away, I promise."

He smiled at her to encourage her response and said, "What would you think of donating some of your older stuffed toys to the local children's hospital? Wouldn't that be a nice thing to do?"

She thought for a moment or two, and while he could see that reaching such a momentous decision was a real struggle for her, she finally said, "Sure, Daddy, I guess that would be okay with me."

"Good girl," he said. "Then let's go through what you have and see what goes and what stays, okay?"

About fifteen minutes later, the two of them had just about dug through to the very bottom of her toy chest when something caught his eye. Reaching down through the few remaining toys, he pulled out a worn-looking, small stuffed owl that had obviously long been adored. It was one of those motion-activated dolls that speaks whenever it's picked up; it gave him a little start when it said, "*Whooo* do you love most of all?"

They both laughed out loud, sharing the surprise of hearing the owl's funny recorded voice. And then, sensing the opportunity to teach his daughter a special lesson, he turned to her and said, "Sweetheart, what was the name you gave to this little owl?"

She was still smiling. "Solomon—that's his name; isn't he the cutest thing you've ever seen?" And she reached up to take him from her father's hand. But he withheld it for a moment, asking, "Seems I remember you telling me more than once that Solomon was your very favorite stuffed animal. Or"—and then, pausing for the briefest of moments, he asked a question designed to have a special impact on her—"maybe that's not true anymore?"

"Oh, no, Daddy, I do—I *do* love Solomon most of all. But I ..." And she came to a stop.

He watched as her young mind struggled to resolve the contradiction in her recent actions, which was exactly the effect he had hoped to achieve by his last question.

"But what, little one?" he said.

"I guess I must've forgotten about him."

Acting as if he was going through the same process of discovery with her, he asked, "Hmmm ... isn't that strange? How do you suppose that you forgot all about Solomon and how much you love him?"

She opened her eyes real wide, like she always did whenever she felt puzzled by something, and then looked up at her father, somehow knowing that he was about to help her see something. He could see the unspoken question in her eyes and her willingness to listen, so he continued.

"Because you had him so covered up with so many other things that you *don't* love anymore, you forgot that he even exists."

His words had just the gentle impact that he hoped they would when, a moment later, she said to him, "Oh, no—that won't do, will it, Daddy?"

Again he smiled to encourage her growing realization. "No, it won't. Now what do you think we can do so that you never again forget your beloved Solomon?"

She smiled back broadly, sensing the truth of all that she was seeing, and said, "When I put my toys away each night before I go to sleep, I must remember to put Solomon on the very top of all of them so that he's never out of sight." And she looked up at him again to see if she was right.

"Yes, my darling. Exactly!"

KEY LESSON

We have no greater friend in life than that small part of us that loves what is true. The more we are able to recognize and honor the fact of this matter, the more powerfully this interior friend steps forward and proves to us the value of our love for it.

A FINAL WORD
OF ENCOURAGEMENT

*The Secret of Being at
Peace with Yourself*

A sports reporter for a large newspaper was assigned to cover an international marathon hosted each year by his city. From past experience, he knew that thousands of people would turn out to test themselves over the grueling twenty-six-mile course; he had also seen ten times that number of people line the streets to cheer them on.

But, as this was the umpteenth time he'd been asked to cover the race, he wanted to do something new. He had already interviewed most of the likely winners more than once and knew their backstories all too well. So he decided that he would cover the race from a different angle; this year's story would be about the person *who finished last.*

As always, the day of the big race began with its official pomp and ceremony, including the usual confusion surrounding the runners' registration booth. Soon thousands of runners wearing brightly colored jerseys with paper numbers pinned to the front and back lined up for the starting gun. And then—bang! They were off!

It was only a little more than two hours later when—setting a record time—the first contestant crossed the finish line to the deafening cheers of admiring fans. As the minutes and hours ticked off the official clock, more and more men and women made their way into the arms of family and friends who had cheered them all along, waiting for them to finish.

Slowly but surely, the throngs of people who had lined the streets faded back into the city's background, returning to their homes, enriched and exhausted by the day's events. The sun was setting by the time the last group of a few runners came walking, some limping, across the finish line. The reporter wanted to go home, but he knew the race wasn't over yet.

It was still several hours later when he spied the last contestant making her way to the final checkpoint. Her body fairly shouted the pain she was in; clearly, every step was a struggle. A wave of compassion swept through him, and for a moment he doubted the wisdom of trying to interview the last runner in the race. Surely she was already suffering enough without being asked what it was like to finish dead last. As she drew closer, he strained to make out some of her features.

At first—due to the dim light cast by the city street lamps—he doubted his own eyes, but as she got closer and closer to where he stood, it looked like she was sporting a big smile across her face. Soon enough he could see that in spite of the occasional involuntary grimace of pain, she was, in fact, quite happy. In spite of being partially bent over with exhaustion, her eyes were bright; something about her spirit was standing there upright, undaunted. He couldn't help but feel strangely drawn to her.

Grabbing one of the sponsor-supplied sport bottles with water in it, he jogged over to the spot where she crossed the finish line and, handing it to her, offered his congratulations.

Thanking him for his kindness, she took a couple long, deep swallows. A moment or two later, he introduced himself as a reporter and asked if he might trouble her with just a couple of questions. To his surprise, she showed no hesitancy, saying, "Of course. What would you like to know?"

Doing his best to make eye contact with her, he hoped she could see that he sincerely wanted to understand how she was feeling; it was important to him at this point—knowing the kind of question he was about to ask—that she realize he wasn't judging her performance. He began:

"Did you know that you're the very last person to finish this race?"

"Yes, that's pretty much what I expected," she said.

"Well, what's that like? I mean, how does it feel?" Again he tried to convey through his eyes that he sincerely wanted to understand her feelings. "Do you have any regrets that out of the thousands who ran this race today, none of them took as much time as you did to reach the finish line?"

She looked down at the ground for a moment, and his heart went out to her; the last thing he wanted her to feel was that he was belittling her or her efforts. But the next moment she looked back up at him, eyes smiling, and said something that he would never forget:

"I'm at peace with myself. Do you want to know why?"

Very much surprised by her question, the reporter said, "Yes, please, by all means. I think all of my readers would like to share your experience here today."

She paused for a moment, obviously collecting her thoughts, and said:

"I ran as hard as I could for as long as I could. So, you see, I have nothing to regret. Besides," she continued, her eyes flashing a certain mischievous glow, "I'm sure I'll do a lot better next year!"

KEY LESSON

When it comes to those who persist with their wish to be free regardless of the cost, the best just keeps unfolding.

ABOUT THE AUTHOR

Best-selling "letting go" author Guy Finley's encouraging and accessible message is one of the true bright lights in our world today. His ideas cut straight to the heart of our most pressing personal and social issues—relationships, success, addiction, stress, peace, happiness, freedom—and lead the way to a higher life. Barnes and Noble says: "Guy Finley has helped millions live fuller, more peaceable lives."

Finley is the acclaimed author of *The Secret of Letting Go* and more than forty other books and audio programs on the subject of self-realization, several of which have become international bestsellers. In addition, he has presented over four thousand unique self-realization seminars to thousands of grateful students throughout North America and Europe over the past thirty years. Each week several hundred thousand subscribers in 142 countries read his popular free newsletter.

His popular works, published in twenty languages, are widely endorsed by doctors, professionals, and religious leaders of all denominations. Among many others, his popular titles include *The Secret of Letting Go, Let Go and Live in the Now, The Courage to Be Free, Apprentice of the Heart, The Essential Laws of Fearless Living, Design Your Destiny,* and *The Intimate Enemy.*

Guy has been a guest on over six hundred television and radio shows, including national appearances on ABC, NBC, CBS, CNN, and NPR, and is currently syndicated on several international radio networks, including Healthylife Radio, Achieve Radio, and World Talk Radio.

In addition to his writing and appearance schedule, Guy is the founding director of Life of Learning Foundation, the renowned nonprofit center for self-study in Merlin, Oregon, where he speaks four times each week on the subject of self-realization. Meetings are ongoing, open to the public, and offered for a suggested donation of three dollars, but no one is turned away.

To contact Guy Finley about this book, write to:

Life of Learning Foundation
P.O. Box 10 IAM
Merlin, OR 97532

You can receive a free starter kit with helpful Guy Finley materials, including a 60-minute MP3 download of Guy's talk "5 Simple Steps to Make Yourself Fearless," access to an online Wisdom Library featuring 75 short and powerful Guy Finley talks, sacred meditation music, Guy's *30 Keys to Change Your Destiny* ebook, and Guy's weekly email newsletter, delivered once a week right to your desktop.

To receive all this free, life-changing material, visit:

www.guyfinley.org/kit

Be sure to visit Guy Finley's award-winning multimedia website at www.guyfinley.org. Enjoy free MP3 downloads and videos, read volumes of published and unpublished works, browse the bookstore, and have free access to a host of other invaluable resources, including frequently asked questions, archived key lessons, and podcasts.

You can also follow Guy Finley on Facebook (www.guyfinley.org/facebook), Twitter (www.guyfinley.org/twitter), and YouTube (www.guyfinley.org/youtube).